FRUGAL LIVING

Your Complete Guide To Saving Money And
Simplifying Your Life

(How to Save Money and Not Feel Like You're
Broke)

Daniel Turman

Published by Harry Barnes

Daniel Turman

All Rights Reserved

Frugal Living: Your Complete Guide To Saving Money And Simplifying Your Life (How to Save Money and Not Feel Like You're Broke)

ISBN 978-1-77485-149-4

Legal & Disclaimer

The information contained in this book is not designed to replace or take the place of any form of medicine or professional medical advice. The information in this book has been provided for educational and entertainment purposes only.

The information contained in this book has been compiled from sources deemed reliable, and it is accurate to the best of the Author's knowledge; however, the Author cannot guarantee its accuracy and validity and cannot be held liable for any errors or omissions. Changes are periodically made to this book. You must consult your doctor or get professional medical advice before using any of the suggested remedies, techniques, or information in this book.

Upon using the information contained in this book, you agree to hold harmless the Author from and against any damages, costs, and expenses, including any legal fees potentially resulting from the application of any of the information provided by this guide. This

Legal & Disclaimer

The information contained in this book is not designed to replace or take the place of any form of medicine or professional medical advice. The information in this book has been provided for educational and entertainment purposes only.

The information contained in this book has been compiled from sources deemed reliable, and it is accurate to the best of the Author's knowledge; however, the Author cannot guarantee its accuracy and validity and cannot be held liable for any errors or omissions. Changes are periodically made to this book. You must consult your doctor or get professional medical advice before using any of the suggested remedies, techniques, or information in this book.

Upon using the information contained in this book, you agree to hold harmless the Author from and against any damages, costs, and expenses, including any legal fees potentially resulting from the application of any of the information provided by this guide. This

Table of Contents

Introduction

Thanks for downloading this book, you will really have a lot of things to learn and I hope you enjoy it!

Chapter 1: What Is Frugal Living?

Frugal living is the art of managing to lead a normal life with the help of minimum possible expenses. It involves useful resource management in a wise manner and encourages spending as less as possible on daily needs.

First, frugal living is about using less money. Money talks; there are rare exceptions to that. For those who have it in abundance; be it through family inheritance or personal means, money is not a problem when it comes to sustain them.

However, for those who do not earn a truckload by the month, sustenance isn't a problem but fulfilling extraneous wishes might be. The latter category people find it difficult to quench their thirst for artful living, as most of their salaries are spent on meeting their monthly ends.

It's also about efficient management. Living frugally is more about managing than spending less. You can always increase your earning capacity by getting a promotion or working harder.

If you are a businessman, you can expand your business and create more opportunities for heightening your income, but what if despite earning more you fail to manage your money effectively? Frugal life isn't just for those earning less bucks; it's about inculcating a habit of saving and learning to live with the help of minimum possible resources.

A frugal lifestyle is also about resistance. Resisting the temptation to give in to your cravings is a vital part of living frugally. If you have the spending capacity, you are bound to get attracted to lavish ways of leading a posh lifestyle.

It's hard to stop your legs carrying you off to the shop displaying 'SALE' at the end of your local market, isn't it? Frugal lifestyle teaches you to say no to such temptations and learn to make peace with your longings. This will not only save you precious money but also teach you how to take control of your life.

Another very important part of a frugal life is the power of selection. There often come situations where we are torn between two equally good choices and we have to choose only one. What we end up doing is selecting both the options. A frugal life teaches us to choose the best one out of the given options. Being able to part with good options is often not easy but we need to make the decision one way or other.

Leading a frugal lifestyle isn't an easy path to tread upon. It not only encourages less spending, but also advocates for wise spending. Despite what one earns, a habit of frugality comes handy for possible dire times and unforeseen circumstances.

Chapter 2: Why Savings Accounts Are Important

It happens. Sometimes things just seem to be going well for the first time since forever. You are asked to bail Aunt Edna out of jail if Uncle Henry is again arrested or someone gets sick.

You can't predict what life will throw at you so it is important to hedge your financial bets. This is best done by opening a savings account.

It is easy to open a savings account. One can open one at any bank or credit union around the globe. You don't even have to leave your home in this modern age. In a matter of minutes, you can open an online savings account.

You probably already have a savings account linked to your checking account. Your bank should offer a free account if you don't have one. If you are using the bank to check your account, the minimum balance is often quite small. Savings accounts may be subject to a fee, so it is worth shopping around.

You put yourself at risk if you stash money under your mattress or in a shoebox up top of your closet. This is especially true if you are saving some money. You could lose all your life savings if someone breaks into your house. Do not be fooled by people who think it won't happen. It does happen, and it can happen in the most beautiful of places to people who believe that this kind of stuff is only for other people.

The Federal Deposit Insurance Corporation (FDIC), covers money in savings accounts up to $250K. You shouldn't read this book if you have more money than $250K. Spread your money across several accounts if you are reading this book for fun.

You can save cash for major emergencies. The new iPhone doesn't count as an emergency. To ensure that you are financially secure enough to weather any emergency, start saving as much money now as you can. Financial experts recommend that you have enough savings to cover six months of your expenses. Although this may not be possible for everyone, aim for three months of savings.

These tips will show you how to save money. Don't waste the money you save on things you don't really need. Instead, place that money in a savings account. Keep it there until you need. You'll soon have enough money to pay the down-payment for that dream house or to send your children to college.

Your savings account should be viewed as a black hole, where money can go in and out. If you have money in savings, it should be kept there until you need it. Save your money for emergencies or if you don't think your children will be able to pay them.

Let me tell you about a friend of mine who I tried for many years to get a savings account. Finally, I was able to get through to her and walk her through how to set up an account. When she said she had completed the process and was ready to save money, I felt proud like a mother.

Fast forward six months. One day, we were talking and she asked me how her savings account was doing. She looked at me sheepishly and said that she had been trying but couldn't save any money. She didn't have a good job, but she did make enough money to be able to stash some away.

To get to the bottom, I began asking probing questions. She was actually putting money away in savings but treating her savings account as an additional checking account. The savings account had a debit card that she used whenever her regular checking account was low. She was not saving money but instead she was putting money into two accounts and then spending it all.

This is an example of how to misuse a savings account. Savings are just that: savings. It is your responsibility to make sure you save money. It's important to save money if you aren't doing so. Even if it's just a few dollars here and there. Although it may not seem like much in the short-term, just a few dollars here and there can add up over time.

To put it into perspective, if you can save 100 bucks per month in an account paying 2 percent interest for 5 years, that will give you $6300 in savings. This amount will double in ten years to nearly $13K. Although it may not appear so, it's more than 100 dollars per month that you could be putting into savings.

The Thirty-Day Rule

People are known for being spontaneous spenders. We buy things we like, no matter how expensive. We are more likely to buy things that cost more than we need. To combat impulse buying, enforce a 30-day rule.

If you are looking for something very expensive, wait 30 days before buying it. The thirty-day period is over, and you should consider whether you need the item or not.

You'll soon realize that you don't really care about the item. You won't feel the urge to purchase on impulse and the item will no longer be as appealing as it was thirty days ago.

The list should be kept in your mind. You'll forget about it more often than you think by the time the list reaches thirty days. This will enable you to keep the important items in your mind and filter out the less important.

You can still purchase any item that passes the 30-day time limit. Consider the pros and cons of each item for a week. Do you really need it or do you just want it? What is the estimated cost of the item? What will it cost to maintain the item's condition? Are there cheaper alternatives? Is the item being purchased for yourself or because it will make you look good to others. There are many things to consider. It's possible to purchase the item if you feel you need it. As long as you can still afford food and bills.

This technique will help you avoid making unnecessary purchases.

Chapter 3: Too Much Clutter

People fill their homes in the same way that they pack for trips, and have more than enough "just in case." This has led to society placing too much emphasis on possessions, believing that they bring happiness or are a sign of success.

You can't measure happiness or success by simply accumulating large quantities of things. The old joke "he who dies first with the most toys wins" is not a valid way to think in this age of "going green". One might even say that the new version of the old saying "he who leaves this world with the most clutter wins" is more accurate.

People are now trying to keep their belongings under 100. This could mean different things to different people. For example, not counting furniture or accepting a collection pots and pans for a "kitchen set" that equals one item.

It is important not to obsess over the wrong or right, but to evaluate what items are filling closets, covering shelves with decorative nick-knacks, or costing money to store in a rented storage space.

You can think of renting an apartment to store stuff you don't use anymore as renting a storage unit. Consider the savings if you were to reduce the cost of storage rental fees.

Storage expenses

You could look at it like this: If it hasn't been used within the last 6 months, it is a keeper. It's not about removing items that may be lost later or moving family heirlooms into the dumpster.

If in doubt, it is best to keep the item. It may become clearer the next time you go through, if it is still worthwhile to keep or if it is ready for a new home.

Nearly everyone has heard the expression, "We don't own our stuff, but our stuff owns you." Nobody on "Hoarders," ever seems happy with the way they live. It's not about cluttering up the house, but about selling, donating, or repurposing items that can be used in a different way.

What do you do with all of this stuff?

Garage sales, eBay and Craig's List are all options. You can also donate to thrift shops or charities that offer sales to raise funds. Spend some time researching to find organizations that may be able to use certain items.

For example, soup kitchens can always use an extra set of plates. Bedding is a constant requirement for animal shelters. It's amazing to see the amount of bedding that charitable organizations require, most of which is in someone's basement or garage.

Always try to get cash first before you buy clothing. It can be easier to let go of something if you have a few dollars than to donate immediately. There's nothing wrong in trying to make a little more of the money you spent on these items. You can resell the items through eBay or at a yard sale.

To avoid clutter, you can let someone else sell the merchandise. The best buy-sell-trade stores like Buffalo Exchange are the best because the cash is available immediately. Consignment shops are the second best option. Although it takes longer to receive any money, getting a check once per month is not bad.

Books - Local used bookstores often use the same buy-sell trade method. This route offers the opportunity to make a profit or get a new book. Another great option is Bookmooch which allows book traders to trade online. To purchase a book from another user, users can list the books they have and use credits earned for this. Libraries are always in desperate need of literature, so don't hesitate to ask.

Toys... Being a parent means that you have toys. However, if clutter is a problem, it's possible to adopt a "out with old, in with new" lifestyle. One way to reduce clutter is to connect with parents and trade age-appropriate toys. Another option is to use online toy swapping sites. Once the child has outgrown the need for toys, it is possible to donate the toys. This will allow you to clear out your home and set an example for future generations. Donation Town is a national organization that accepts donations.

However, this does not mean you should stop shopping.

When shopping for a new item, the best strategy is to keep one thing out and put one in. This means that you have to get a new shirt and let go of the one you already own. This approach is applicable to almost all kinds of belongings. Another thing to think about is why you are shopping.

There is no doubt that something is essential. You should use common sense if you are unsure about the item. It might be worth sleeping on the item before you make a purchase. It might be a good idea to sleep on it before you buy. There are many ways to determine whether certain items are worth buying.

Each dollar saved is worth every item that isn't bought impulsively. The majority of purchases bring temporary happiness. A trinket that takes up $20 could be used to pay for a class in yoga or a pedicure. The resulting euphoric high lasts longer and is more healthy than the one you get from buying it. The self-esteem building power of saving money and the pride it brings is unmatched.

Chapter 4: Shopping

Shop after major holidays

The biggest savings are often after major holidays. After Christmas there's Boxing Day and of course in the US there is Black Friday and Cyber Monday sales. These are great times to search for great deals and for future presents.

Corporate Discounts

I already mentioned company benefits but while this is similar it's a little different. Did you know that bigger companies often have some sort of discount program with other companies? This could be for shopping, financial services, event tickets, etc. Ask around and see if your company has something similar. Not everything will be a great deal but there might be something that could save you some decent money, always remember to shop around! At my last company they were part of a bigger discount program and I could save money on all sorts of things including discounts on flights, car rentals, car purchases, and much more!

Get a Rain check

If you find an advertised product that was an amazing deal but sold out, get a rain check. This way if the product is back in stock you'll be able to get the item for the price advertised and won't lose out. Not every store will do this for you but it's always worth taking the time to ask if it's that good of a deal.

Unsubscribe from shopping site e-mail lists

While I did tell you to enrol in reward programs and their e-mail list, some sites will only send you promotional material. These sites will send you "great deals" and "sales" e-mails, which will inevitably lead to impulse purchases down the road. Unsubscribe from them so won't by that lime green sweater that you'll never wear, even though it's 80% off. If this is the case, unsubscribe from these e-mail lists asap!

Don't fall for the 3-for-2 "trick"

I always roll my eyes when I see this promotion. "Buy 3 shoes for the price of 2" First off, why on Earth would I need 3 shoes and second of all, it's not a good deal at all. It's a way for the store to increase their revenue by making you think it's a great deal. Sure it might seem like a sale, but you're going to end up with two extra pairs of shoes that you really don't need and likely won't even wear.

Avoid Extended Warranties

This is one of the greatest way for companies to make money, which on the flip side means it's one of the worst ways for you to spend your money. Extended warranties are expensive and actually don't cover everything. Don't let the salesperson trick you, most of them don't even know the full contents of the extended warranties and are only worried about the nice commission they get for each extended warranty sale. These warranties are also constructed so that they expire right before the item in question breaks. It's a numbers game, heavily tilted in their favor, avoid extended warranties!

Buy used books versus new books

Amazon and eBay are great places to find pretty much every used book. Another great website that my professor introduced me to back in undergrad was addall.com, this site let's you punch in the title, author, ISBN, etc. of a book and does a search for used book sites worldwide and includes the shipping and handling fees (where applicable) so that you can find the best deal.

Use Online Coupons

You'll find coupons for pretty much everything from webhosting, domain names, clothes, freebies and more. Check out sites like retailmenot.com before making any purchase or simply do a Google search for "name of store coupon" and you're bound to find something.

Buy discounted gift cards for shopping

Many people receive gift cards that they don't want and decide to sell them to sites like CardPool.com, GiftCardGranny.com or even eBay. If you know you're going to buy something from a specific retailer use your rewards credit card (to rack up the points) to buy a gift card at a discount and even better yet, use online coupons and buy something on sale from that retailer!

Sign up and use online rebate sites

If you're going to make purchases online, why not utilize sites like Ebates.com and get cash back for your purchases? For signing up, Ebates will give you a bonus and you can even get rebates on sites like Amazon! You'll find a ton of other online retailers that you can also purchase from and therefore get cash back from. There's no reason not to utilize sites like Ebates to save a little extra!

Don't Shop with Friends

Taking friends on your shopping trips is asking for trouble. If they buy something, you'll want something too. You'll likely try something on that you had no plan of buying and they will persuade you into buying it since in their mind it's a great deal. While it might be fun shopping with friends, it isn't financially smart unless you have a friend that will dissuade you from buying anything at all, in that case take them with you every time you go shopping!

Search on eBay for anything specific before paying retail price

If you're looking to buy something specific then do a quick search on eBay.com. Chances are there'll be someone selling that item and that person might have bought the wrong model, size, color you name it and be selling it for a steep discount to the retail price. Sure you might not that be lucky but it's worth a shot, I've bought many things on eBay and saved quite a bit of money.

Make a list of items that you want and stick to it!

Impulse purchases kill our budget and savings. We see something that seems like a great deal and the store makes you believe that it'll be the last time you'll be able to purchase it. But it turns out a day or two later you see the same item for an even better deal, or you could have bought the item online and saved even more.

If you're disciplined and make a list of items that you really want it'll prevent impulse purchases. This isn't a list of items that are necessities, they're actual items that you want. Yes, put the $800 pair of Christian Louboutins for the ladies or a new Macbook Pro, TV, vacation, or even a new dishwasher. Put all the items on the list so that you know what you want, and if it didn't the make the list then you clearly don't need it, just be reasonable with yourself please. And the key is to save money before making some of these purchases.

Don't buy just because it's on sale!

We're all guilty of this. We buy something just because it's on sale and seems like a great deal. But it turns out after a few months you realize that you have stuff in your closet that you've never worn or used. Sound familiar?

Impulse purchases are the worst and I'm still guilty of this on a regular basis. If you really need to buy something plan for it beforehand. For example, create a list of items that you need and want and think it through before pulling out the credit card. If you let a decision sit for 24 hours, sometimes what seemed like a great deal won't appear as appealing. Trust me, you'll always find another pair of beautiful shoes that will be 75% off. It won't be the last pair, I assure you!

Find daily best deals on sites like fatwallet.com

If you have some necessities around the home or have an item on the "want" list that you want to buy and have saved for, then checking on sites like fatwallet.com or eBay's daily deals might be a great place to check on a regular basis. The key here is "if" you can control yourself from impulse purchases, as there will be "great" deals everyday.

Buy bulk for items that you'll definitely use

There's no question that by buying bulk you'll save money when you consider the price per item. But that doesn't mean you should be buying everything in bulk just because it might seem like a better deal. Let's talk about some of the things you'll want to buy in bulk.

Items that have long shelf life such as pasta, dried fruits, and cereal (kind of). Did you know there was a website dedicated to shelf life? Shelflifeadvice.com is a great resource to see what will have a longer shelf life.

Other items that you can buy in bulk to save money:

• Alcohol (Boxed wine or a case of beer)

• Toilet paper, tissue paper, and paper towels

• Toothbrushes

• Supplements: Vitamins and other supplements

• Diapers

Just to name a few, we all have different needs in our lives so if you have something that you use quite often and can save money by buying bulk then you should! You obviously have to pay more upfront but you'll save more money in the long run.

Be organized to avoid duplicate purchases

Have you gone to the store and bought extra vegetables, fruits, or shampoo forgetting that you already had some at home? I'm sure you've done it, I certainly have, and it's because well for one, we're all very busy and have better things to think about. But it's also because sometimes we get a little disorganized and it can be hard to stay on top of what we do and don't have at home. By being organized in general we'll have a better grasp of what we have at home. Start with your refrigerator!

Take Advantage of Birthday Freebies and Gifts

Pretty much every retailer gives you something free and/or a discount on your birthday. Whether if it's a free drink at Starbucks or x% off at your favorite retailer, these are great times to save a little extra money.

Buy Refurbished Items

Did you know that many retailers, even Apple, sell items that are refurbished? Refurbished simply means that an item that was brand new was returned to the vendor or manufacturer for any reason, if there was a problem it has been fixed and is basically "like new". You could save a significant amount by using this tactic.

Chapter 5: What happened to me

It wasn't as if everything was fine. My company, which I worked for, didn't recover from 2008's financial crisis and was forced to close. I lost my job. I didn't have much money to fall back on. My life and my situation required me to reorganize. It was very difficult to find jobs in ever-laboring occupations. To keep up with everything, I sold everything I didn't use in the weekend markets to make ends meet. This was not very lucrative. While I did have a few odd jobs, nothing was permanent. I was too expensive to live in the city so I moved out to a small town in the country where rents were much cheaper. Part-time work on farms was my only source of income. That kept me going, and it brought in some extra money.

This is where I can start a garden. Before, I couldn't. I had been doing internet research for some time so that helped. Although I still did the markets, it was more of a hobby. I was familiar with all the free and cheap places to eat. There was a savings when I collected driftwood to make firewood. I reduced my purchases and went to the charity shops for anything that I didn't need. It was small and didn't require much gas, which saved me a lot of money. Most importantly, I began to meet people and build my network. Volunteer work at the radio station and in the country garden helped me to feel more comfortable.

This book describes how I reinvented myself to "Save Money Doing Internet Jobs From Home and Living Frugally." It is not something I wanted, but I had to. It can be hard to live without a steady income. The government and tax payers deserve my gratitude for their social welfare programs. Without them, I would be in serious trouble.

What's happening now

The world is in 2020. It has completely changed from when I was a child. The government has gone crazy with regulation and tax. The internet adds to the cost. Rents are not cheap and electricity prices continue to rise. You can also be sure that land taxes will rise if you've made the largest investment in your life, and have actually bought a house. While the world has changed, so has the cost of gas. It would be reasonable to expect that the government would offer some tax relief for gas, but this would leave them with less money to waste. All sides are being screwed. Let's not forget milk. While the world has seen a drop in the price of milk, the price on the supermarket shelves has not changed.

While all expenses have increased, wages and pensions have not. The home front is not doing well. You remember your parents saving money and you would love to continue it. But there's nothing left at the end. It's easy to let money slip through your fingers. Even if you are employed, you should still have a plan for saving money.

You cannot afford to have any financial problems if you live paycheck to paycheck. The cost of food has risen to an all-time high. Anyone who is tight on their budget can no longer afford bread and butter. You must keep track of how much money slips through you fingers in order to survive.

Rent is the most expensive expense, and it comes out every week. This is the first expense, and there isn't much else. How do you get cheap rent? One man I know lives in a van. He only pays for the space in a covered and locked garage. This is much cheaper than renting a room or apartment. You will need to ask around to find out what each place has to offer. It can take a while to learn about a place. He was able to find all the bathrooms, where to get a shower, and the cost of $2. There were also all the community centers that gave out food and churches. He loved living very cheaply and he enjoyed it. He lived in a garage that was very run-down and had enough space for 30 cars. But he could use the entire place after work. Not everyone can afford to do this. But what if you have a family? He was all by himself.

Every month, expenses such as water and electricity have increased dramatically. The internet has created a new monthly expense that must be paid. This was a monthly expense that was only paid once a month 10 years ago. It could be called a modern expense. The internet has made it possible to get rid of cable and TV. You can also forgo the daily newspapers and books. There are some savings.

Everyone talks about budgeting. I just try to keep track of everything. I keep receipts for everything and add them all up at the end. This is in addition to all other expenses like the car. This is an additional expense to all other monthly expenses. You can stop money from going stale by knowing where it goes. Keep all receipts and find out where it is going. It is very difficult to budget when you live money in and money out. You also have to consider yearly expenses such as taxes, which can sneak up on your budget and are not cheap. What can you do to budget when there is nothing?

Health care, particularly for dentists, is another major expense. It pays to shop around for dentists, as there are many affordable options. One that I used to use was run by a church group. It was quite affordable, although I had to pay. There are amazing prices for dental work. But there are also incredibly expensive prices. So do your research. You could make an appointment at the university so that the students studying dentistry could treat your teeth. They were competent as long as they were properly supervised. You didn't put your teeth in anyone's hands. It's a good idea to take care of your teeth when you live on a budget. Mixing baking soda with hydrogen peroxide helps me keep a toothache under control. I floss because it helps.

It is easy to make changes, but it can be difficult to stick to them. This is not something you can do if you aren't ready. You will be resisted by your children and spouse. You have to take it slowly. If you're walking by a second-hand shop or church charity shop, stop and take a look. These places can be quite expensive so make sure you check the prices in department stores. With all the discounts available in shops, it is often cheaper to purchase what you need on a special. Don't buy impulse. You can plan what you want to purchase. Ask yourself if you really need it. If so, continue looking for it second-hand or on special.

Chapter 6: First Person: How I Set Goals

To Get What I Want

During the years, I have had the good fortune of being able to advance my education and financial stature. That didn't happen over night. Nor did it happen without a plan. After a few younger years of spinning my wheels, I decide it's all about setting goals. Here's how I set goals to get what I want.

• What's Worthy of a Goal?

Why set a goal? If you just work hard, you'll get what you want eventually, right? That's what I thought as a youngster. It didn't take me long to see that my lofty ambitions wouldn't take flight without a goal and a plan to accompany it.

When I first starting setting goals, I only set them for really big things – like buying a car or a house. But, then I realized that nothing else seemed to materialize and my other dreams just seemed to extend from year-to-year as just that – a dream. The house was purchased, but it had no furniture. The car was in the driveway, but it wasn't driving to me vacation destinations once a year as I had hoped.

I finally figured out that for anything I wanted, I needed to set a goal in my life. Big or small, I needed to lay it out with a stated outcome, timeline, budget and a plan to get there. So I also started planning the small purchases, vacations, projects and charity work I wanted to accomplish. That was the beginning of my five year plan.

• My Five Year Plan

Once I realized planning was my best vehicle for success, I also realized that I couldn't do it all in one year. I had so many things to get and accomplish; it wasn't really possible to do them all in one year. Funny, once I figured that out, I actually gave myself a little breathing room.

When I laid out everything I desired on paper – it was usually one big, long list. When I kept this list in my head in the past, I didn't have the proper mechanism to size it. Therefore, all it symbolized was a long list of things I wanted, but didn't get. Without a plan, I didn't have a chance. Unfortunately, it made me feel a little like a failure when I made the same New Years resolutions year-on-year. Having a long term plan, however, helped me understand realistic limitations and how to work with them.

I create a five year plan every year – right around Thanksgiving time. It just seems like a natural time to reflect, be thankful for the things I have and be hopeful for the future. It may sound silly to create a five year plan every year; but the truth is – things change and I change my plans accordingly. So each year, I make a list of where I want to be at the end of the coming year and for each of four years after that. From vacations to starting a new hobby or business – every item I desire gets incorporated into my five year plan.

• Yearly, Monthly, Weekly and Daily Goals

Once I have my five year plan in place, everything else falls into place naturally. I concentrate on my first year with a fever – but, I'm always mindful of anything I need to set up for the coming year.

I set monthly, weekly and daily budgets and "to do" lists that all support my yearly plan. And as each day, week, month and year progresses, it all fits together. I get so much more accomplished than I ever did before I set goals.

Do I get everything I want? In a word, "No." But, I usually get pretty darn close. And should I not accomplish a goal in a given year, I just make sure I roll it forward at Thanksgiving when I create my new five year plan. What can I say? It may sound like a lot of planning; but, it works for me.

Chapter 7: Random Tools Used To Save

Money

There are many tools I use to get the best pricing on the items I buy. I made a list of the ones I use the most throughout the year, and I invite you to try one or all of these. I can guarantee that incorporating these tools into your daily financial habits will save you money throughout the year, perhaps even hundreds of dollars. I won't lie, it's difficult even for me to save the most on every single purchase I make. Sometimes you are going to miss out on the best deal, and that's okay. Sometimes you are going to prioritize convenience over saving a few bucks, and that's also okay. Other times, saving $100 can come down to being patient and waiting a week or two if you know your item is going to be on sale. If you want to buy a laptop and Black Friday is right around the corner (and yours is still working), then you should just wait. Things change a little if you are without a laptop and need one ASAP (but even then, there are ways to ensure you aren't overpaying).

One of the ideas behind this book is that by using some money-saving tricks you will be able to save or recoup on your everyday purchases. With some luck, you will be able to stop living paycheck to paycheck and might even set up a savings account. Receiving so much information can be overwhelming, and that's why the last part of this book is dedicated to examples on how I approach different purchases and how I use these tools to help me save the most amount of money. The last thing I will mention before diving into the description of each tool is that sometimes you'll only be saving pennies per purchase, but over the year that can add up to hundreds of dollars.

Credit card points

I have been taking advantage of credit card points since I got my first card at the age of 18. The trick to maximizing credit card rewards is to pay your balance every month. Making a minimum payment on your card will undoubtedly lead to the accrued interest on the remaining balance wiping out any benefit you get from earning points.

Here's a quick example of this: One time my mom was going to make a $10,000 house repair. I told her I would pay for it with my card (and earn 1% cash back) and would immediately use the cash she was going to use to pay off my credit card. By doing this, I would end up with 10,000 points (worth $100) on a purchase that was going to happen anyways. Easy money, right? Well, if I had let the $10,000 balance sit on the account for a billing cycle, I would have paid $108.25 in interest that first month (assuming a very low 12.99% APR on the credit card). I would have still earned the $100 in rewards, but I would have had to pay $108.25 in interest. Two billing cycles would have been around $216.50 in interest.

Transaction: $10,000 (house repair cost) x 0.01 (1% cash back on card) = $100 (or 10,000 points)

1st month with outstanding balance: $10,000 (house repair cost) x 0.01 (1% cash back on card) − ($10,000 [balance] x .1299 [12.99% APR on credit card] / 12 months) = $100 − $108.25 = -$8.25

The point is that as long as you use your credit card responsibly, racking up the points can give you a great payout at the end of the year. I personally cash out around $200 every year from using my 1% credit card for most of my everyday purchases.

Let's crunch the numbers on my own spending habits. Currently I purchase around $1,300 with my card every month and pay it off before the billing cycle ends (meaning I make a payment of the full balance once a month). I earn 1% cash back (1 point per $1 spent). Now comes the math to prove that I earn over $100 in points each year.

Points earned per year: $1,300 (average spent per month) x 12 months year x 0.01 (1% cash back) = $156. My card has some categories that earn 3% cash back, so at the end of the year my cash back total is a little bit higher than $156.

I'm thinking about changing to a card that earns 1.5% cash back on every purchase. Let's see how much I would make throughout the year if I made this change.

Changing cards: $1,300 (average spent per month) x 12 months year x 0.015 (1.5% cash back) = $234.

Numbers don't lie. It might be that my Burger King meal only earned me 10 points (equal to 10 cents), but getting in the habit of paying for your everyday purchases with your credit card can accumulate to hundreds of dollars in points throughout the year. I know I am repeating myself, but repetition is essential to forming new habits.

Ibotta

I learned about this little gem a year ago thanks to my couponing adventure. I kept seeing Ibotta mentioned in the couponing app that I was using (Krazy Coupon Lady, which I will talk about later on), and I decided to give it a shot. In the first two months of successfully couponing I was able to recoup more than $100 using Ibotta. This is money that I would've missed out on without the app.

This is the way the app works. You make an account and search through their endless store-specific deals. For example, there might be a cash back offer that's only valid if you buy a Gillette razor at Walmart and not at Target. I used Ibotta the most at Target, Walgreens, and Walmart. Once you find an item that you were going to buy anyways (buying stuff you don't need is just wasting money, unless it's free after rebates), then you look at the description. The only reason to buy something you don't "need" is if it's really cheap and you wanted to try it out anyways. Looking at the description of the deal is important because sometimes the coupon is only valid on certain sizes or count-size. If the item is a match, then you pay for it and simply scan the receipt into the Ibotta app. They apply a credit you're your account almost immediately, and once you reach $20 you can cash out to your bank account—or you can just let your balance grow.

The beauty of Ibotta is that you can use it on top of other in-store coupons. Krazy Coupon Lady does a great job of explaining how to stack coupons to get incredible prices on brand-name items. Sometimes you can even make money from "buying" a certain item (she calls these deals MoneyMakers or MMs).

Ibotta can also be used for purchases online, but I haven't taken advantage of this part of the app since I don't buy online that often. One of the newest features I love is the ability to pay in-store with Ibotta to earn extra cash back. It's only available in some stores, but it's still free money. The last section of the book will have examples of how I navigate through a purchase using Ibotta and other tools together to maximize the amount I save.

Rakuten

This was formerly Ebates, and you might have heard of either name. I have been using it for years, but to a much lesser extent. It's a great way to save money on online purchases, but as I stated before I seldom buy things online. One of the nice things is that they have developed a Chrome extension that installs on your browser and tells you when you're on a website that earns cash back. I have it set up to be annoyingly present, and when I click on the notification it initiates a shopping session for me (earning me cash back on the Rakuten account).

There are other websites and apps that provide similar cash back rewards when doing online shopping. I have just stuck with Rakuten because it's the first one I used and I have been loyal to it. They have a wide array of stores in their repertoire and throw promotions all the time. Their promotions usually involve doubling, tripling, or even quadrupling the percentage you get back from shopping at certain online stores. You can cash out once you earn more than $5 in cash back or wait for them to send out a "Big Fat Check" at the end of the quarter. The $5 threshold is easily doable if you shop online a lot.

Don't forget that Rakuten offers a referral bonus, so if you try it and like it tell your friends and you could both be getting some extra cash (just one more way to earn more with your everyday shopping and by being nice).

Krazy Coupon Lady

I discovered this website when I got it in my head that I wanted to give couponing a try. At first it was very confusing, but within a few hours I was able to understand the system they use to explain the deals. Couponing does require a little effort on your part and the savings are sometimes not worth it to some people, but I loved doing it. I moved to Puerto Rico recently and have been unable to use most of the deals in this website/app, but I still browse it every once in a while to see if there are any deals I can take advantage of on the island.

When I was on my couponing venture, I was able to get nearly $500 worth of products for $140ish. This was after coupons, store rewards, Ibotta savings, and credit card points. The best part was that most of the things I bought were brand name items that I got at the same price or lower than the generic alternatives. I remember one time I was able to get eight Colgate toothpastes at Walgreens for free after using some coupons and Ibotta.

Couponing is a great way to save money IF you use it to buy items you know you will use. I warn you, it's easy to get hooked on searching for deals and stocking up (I would know, I ended up with 150 tide pods and 20 tubes of toothpaste). The other great thing is that sometimes the price is so low that it entices you to try a product or brand that you wouldn't normally buy. I bought my fiancé probably $100 worth of makeup (spent close to $10 after coupons and other savings). She managed to find new brands that she had never thought about using.

If you decide to include couponing into your financial habits, know that it will take some time to learn. In my case, it was totally worth spending the time to do it, but you might not feel the same way. The easiest stores (and the ones I stuck to couponing at) are Target, Walgreens, Rite Aid, and Walmart. I didn't have a CVS in my state, but it's also a very easy store to coupon at and has great deals. Walmart was my least favorite, since they can be very picky when a coupon doesn't scan. Target was normally really nice about accepting coupons that applied to the product I was trying to buy but wouldn't scan for some reason (like if your printer ink is a little wonky).

Couple more things I will mention about couponing and Krazy Coupon Lady before moving to the next section. Sometimes it's worth it to stock up (like candy around Halloween and Easter, decorations a few days after a holiday, some items that don't go on sale that often). I've gotten in the habit of stocking up on chocolate in the weeks before and after Halloween (about 10 bags), and make these last a few months. It doesn't really go bad and I can save around $30 or more doing this since it's candy I was going to buy anyways. If you are going to be couponing, the items that are constantly getting coupons include some shampoo brands, all sorts of makeup, laundry detergent, toothpaste, toothbrushes, and deodorant.

Store ads

You probably only notice the store ads once you get to the store. If you frequent a certain grocery store, I would recommend looking at the ad before driving over there, and adding any deals you like to your list. That way you won't forget them. Tips on saving at the store include getting fruits and vegetables that are in season, look at the prices of the things you are buying (this sounds dumb, but it's easy to grab something simply because it looks good), and make sure that everything gets scanned correctly. It's easiest to fix mistakes when you are at the register than afterwards. Catching a mistake later on involves going to the customer service area, waiting your turn, and explaining everything. Most of the time the people working at customer service were able to resolve any issue and either gave me cash back or explained why the coupon or deal wasn't valid (for example, sometimes I just grabbed the wrong brand).

I was hooked on energy drinks for a while and would wait for them to be on sale. Regular price on the brand I liked was around $2. When there was a 10 for $10 special, I would get up to 40 cans for a savings of $40 (this was an item that I was likely going to buy). Another stock-worthy item is cans of soda around the time of the Super Bowl weekend. You wouldn't believe how excited I got every

Wednesdays, when the new Fred Meyer ad came out.

One last thing about using store ads (specifically for grocery stores). Don't be afraid to try out the generic products to see if you like them. I will use Fred Meyer (a Kroger subsidiary) as an example. I saw that Fred Meyer cheese was seemingly always on special and would sometimes cost as little as $1.25 per 8oz package of shredded cheese. Kraft and Borden on the other hand never seemed to dip below $2 per bag even when they were on special. If you don't eat cheese or if you only eat one package every other month, then these savings don't matter. However, for us (my fiancé and I) it came to savings of $1 every two weeks or $24 per year (if compared to the name brand's sale price , which wasn't guaranteed).

I know that $2 per week doesn't seem impressive, but adding up the savings of all the products I bought the generic brand for (without sacrificing taste) came out to $100 or more in savings throughout the year. The idea is that you should try a generic brand at least once. If you don't like it then you lost a couple of bucks. If you don't notice a difference over the brand you usually buy, then you could save hundreds of dollars throughout the years.

Groupon/LivingSocial

Depending on the area you live in, Groupon and LivingSocial can be great tools to save money. If you are unfamiliar with these sites then listen up. You create an account with them and they will provide you with a number of discounts on activities, food, and other things around you. I used Groupon the most for discounts on food and on massages. Depending on your budget and how flexible you are about trying a new place, the savings can be up to 90% (usually between 30%-50%).

It's excellent when you find a place that you frequent. For example, I lived in Oregon and really liked going to a place called Muchas Gracias. Browsing the

LivingSocial promotion email I saw that this restaurant was on the list and offered $30 worth of vouchers for $15. I jumped on that 50% discount and enjoyed great food at a great price (and saved myself $15 that I would have otherwise spent, since I wasn't going to stop going to Muchas Gracias). I've also used Groupon for dance lessons once (they retailed for $200 and I got them for $20), laser hair removal (6 sessions for $100), movie theater voucher ($10 for $20 worth), and much more.

Rewards programs

If your usual hang out spot has a rewards program, then do yourself a favor and sign up! These rewards programs are almost always free and the rewards they give can be pretty decent. If you go to these places often, then you might as well get rewarded for being a repeat customer. I will make a list of a few of my favorite rewards programs and the things I know they offer at the time of writing this book. Their promotions can change, so keep that in mind. Also, it's possible that they offer more than what's written here and I just didn't know about the other perks

Papa John's – they recently changed their point structure, but pretty much they give you points on every dollar spent on purchases. If you find yourself ordering pizza from them often (either for yourself or for office parties), then signing up for their program is totally worth it. The new point system makes it pretty easy to save enough points to get a free pizza or side. If you are on their mailing list, you will also get special codes in your email that are worth using.

Red Robin – if you go to Red Robin more than twice a year, then you probably know about their awesome Free Burger on your Birthday deal. You do have to be a member of their rewards program, but on the month of your birthday they will give you one free burger. You can cash in your burger any day of your birth month (not only on your actual birthday). The deal applies to nearly any burger (including some of their specialty burgers). Being part of the rewards program also makes you eligible for nearly weekly discounts. For example, all of last summer kids ate for $2.99 on Wednesdays.

Buffalo Wild Wings – another free rewards program that is totally worth it. You can earn extra points for going there during lunch, and you also earn points based on your final bill. You do need to log in to your account and tell the app that you are at the restaurant. You'll also need to scan your receipt at the end of your meal. However, I earned enough points in about 4 visits to get a free burger or an appetizer. My fiancé and I would usually go on Tuesdays and take advantage of their half off on wings. We'd get a large order (20 wings) and would sometimes have a beer with the meal (other times water). It would end up being a great date night that would cost around $15-$20 (including tip).

Target, Walgreens, Rite Aid – all of these stores have free rewards programs that are totally worth it because they make you eligible for their discounted prices. However, Walgreens also gives you points (which you can really rack up if you follow Krazy Coupon Lady or any other couponing blog). Target also throws extra specials that are only available for members of the free rewards program. Furthermore, Target has an added perk of 5% discount if you pay with their Target brand credit card or 1% cash back on all purchases if you are a rewards member (as long as you input your rewards info at the register).

Slickdeals.net

There are many sites like it, but I will mention this site because it's one of the first ones that I found and liked. Pretty much it's a forum that posts great deals that people have found and that you can take advantage of. You can open an account with them and set up notifications for items that you are adamant you need to have, but I personally browse the site whenever I am bored or when I am looking for deals on a specific item (like a laptop).

One of the great things about this site is that it has a free forum where people can post anything, including system errors that benefit the client. One time there was a system error at Home Depot in which they were giving out a $300 discount on various Milwaukee tools. I ended up getting a cordless drill, two extra batteries and charger, and a huge flashlight for $30. It should have been $330, but with the $300 discount I only paid $30.

Whenever I know there is a big purchase in my future, I usually browse Slickdeals first. Most of the time I will find something, sometimes I come up empty handed. Depending on the urgency I have for the item, sometimes I browse the site for up to a month in case something pops up. There are new deals added to the site every day, and they are pretty good about explaining the deal itself (if there's a mail-in rebate, if there's a coupon code you need to enter, if it's only for members that have a certain credit card).

Price Matching

Price matching is your friend! Stores that offer price matching (to certain degrees) include Walmart, OfficeDepot, and Target. The latter is the best price matching store I have every dealt with. I'm not sure if things differ in other states, but the Targets in Oregon were always really nice about price matching within their policy (always read up on the store's policies before trying to price match). Reading up on the policy is important because Target's policy explicitly says that you can't price match eBay prices. However, you can price match MOST Amazon items. This is great if you know there's an item cheaper on Amazon or at Walmart, but the Target is closer to your house and you'd rather just drive to Target. Simply show them proof that the item is cheaper at the other store and that it's in stock, and they will adjust the price at the register.

They even price match when an item is cheaper on their own website. Thanks to Krazy Coupon Lady, I used this trick a few times. More than once I went to a physical Target store for an item that was $2 cheaper on Target.com. I simply showed the person at the register the price on the website and they adjusted the price. Depending on where you live, you might have to push them a little bit on this policy. For example, in Puerto Rico the price matching policy still applies at OfficeDepot but they fought me a lot when I tried to ask them for a price adjustment on an item.

Keep in mind that for a price match to be successful you need to be talking about the same item. This means that it has to be the same brand and model. For example, if Walmart has the Lenovo Flex 5 with an Intel i5 on sale and you are trying to price match at OfficeDepot who has the Lenovo Flex 5 with an AMD Ryzen processor, this won't work. No matter how much you huff and puff, they are completely within their rights to refuse the price match.

Google

If I was at the store and found an item that I felt was too expensive, I would use my phone to look it up on Google. In the US, Google has a tab called Shopping and this will find the item online. It will also tell you if it's cheaper somewhere and this can be used for price matching. This was a last resort for me as it often yielded no lower pricing , but it might work in a pinch. Most of the time I would search for the item on the Amazon, Walmart, and Target websites. If it wasn't cheaper there, I was likely not going to find it cheaper anywhere.

Store scanners/apps

Let's say you are at Target (a store known to have a good price matching policy) and you want to see if Walmart has the same shampoo for cheaper. Simply open up the Walmart app and go to the search function. There is a barcode icon that opens up the camera and lets you scan the items barcode. It instantly looks for the item at Walmart and tells you the price. If it's lower than the Target price, you've got yourself a price match situation.

The scanner tool is also available in Ibotta, and it's great when you aren't sure if an item qualifies for the current promotion. Simply open up Ibotta, go to the barcode scanner icon, and the camera will open. Scan the barcode and it will instantly tell you whether you're holding the item eligible for cash back.

Stocking up

There are times that you are faced with the decision of whether or not to buy in bulk. If it's something that you go through on a large scale, then it's a no brainer. This is where Costco and Sam's club may come in handy. Buying at Costco isn't always cheaper though. If you catch a good sale, you could be getting Chobani yogurt at your grocery store at the same price you pay at Costco. The perk is that at the grocery store you can get the flavors you want and the amounts you want (preventing you from throwing away the yogurts you couldn't eat in time because you bought the Costco-size).

Another time stocking up isn't worth it is when you're buying a spice or a product for a recipe that you'll likely only make once. Let's say the recipe calls for cooking wine, but you never use cooking wine for any other recipe. Let's make up a scenario in which the 6oz bottle of this wine is $4 but the 18oz bottle is $6. You only need 2oz for your recipe... If you know deep down that you're just going to put it in the cupboard and not touch it again, then just buy the 6oz bottle. Now let's think about another scenario. You find a couple of recipes that will use the same cooking wine. Then by all means buy the larger bottle, because you will save yourself some money in the long run (3 small bottles would come to $12 vs $6 for the bigger one).

You should stock up on non-perishable items when you see them on special. I know we don't know each other that well, but I am going to go into TMI territory with the next example. I tried the Charmin super soft toilet paper when Costco had a $5 off coupon on the huge pack and loved it. It wasn't much of a gamble, since Costco has a pretty good return policy and if I didn't like it I could return it (it would've been a little awkward, but I would have done it in the name of savings). Anyways, I liked it and had enough to last me a few months. A couple of months later (when I still had 10 rolls left), I saw that Costco came out with the coupon again. Naturally, I bought another pack. After all, TP doesn't go bad and I know I would be using it. This is an example of when it's worth it to stock up.

When deciding whether or not to stock up, just be honest with yourself when you are comparing prices. If your past experiences see you throwing away food because you bought the big pack and couldn't go through it quick enough, then don't make the same mistake. Saving money per oz or per pound isn't really saving if you are throwing things away because they expired.

Chapter 8: Benefits Of Living Frugal

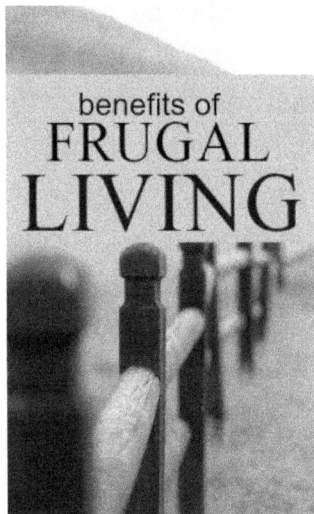

There has been a lot of talk on living frugally and you may be wondering what is so great about it and why many people are choosing it. Being frugal has a positive impact on your finances in a great way and once you discover its benefits, it will be hard not to practice it.

Living frugally is also about making correct and informed choices with regards to whatever you are buying. You are able to live a lifestyle that otherwise would be impossible to achieve. The fact that you spend less might mean that you can even work less. It also helps you to reduce debt or avoid it completely and be able to save money.

Studies have shown that money is one of the leading causes of stress in or lives and if you simplify this relationship then a huge level of stress will be lifted off your shoulders. If you are considering going frugal then these are the advantages you will enjoy.

1.   Having money for emergencies

The truth is that many unexpected things happen. For example, your car may break down, you may need a new water heater or you might even find yourself needing medical attention and these are things we normally do not include in our budget or don't have money for. No matter the kind of emergency you get, the fact that you are living frugally means you have saved up for that. This can give you a great peace of mind.

2.   Do away with fake friends

Almost anyone can wish to go watch a football game with you, go to new clubs, shopping and so on but it takes a true friend to enjoy eating a homemade dinner prepared in your house while enjoying a game of cards. Living a frugal lifestyle may make you lose some friends but the good news is that those who will stick around will be your real friends.

3.   You will waste less

The truth is that we make room for so many junk in our lives and being frugal can prevent you from doing this. When you buy less then you will waste less and frugality involves only buying the things that you truly need and want. You can either buy fewer items or go for used ones. The point is that you will add fewer items to the junk you have. When there is less waste then we will be doing our environment a great justice.

4.   Ability to retire

If you practice frugality for a long period of time then you can be able to retire at some point. Have you ever thought of relaxing at home, travelling or enjoying your hobbies while your age mates work past their 70s? It's a good feeling and this can be possible if you know how to save money because you will have enough for the kind of life you want to live.

5.   Fewer marital problems

It is common knowledge that money is the cause of many marital problems and divorces. Therefore when you become frugal and are on the same page concerning being smart with regard to your money then this will reduce the arguments and therefore the problems you have. You will be able to pay your bills on time, you will have your money in the bank and the level of stress and hostility will greatly lessen. It may sound weird but you might even be surprised at how you can accommodate some of the usually annoying habits of your spouse when you are same page on finances.

6.   Better sleep

Many people leading frugal lives can attest to the fact that they are able to sleep better. This is because there are fewer things to worry about and money is not on that list. At the back of your mind, you are aware of the bills that are due and their dates and the best part is that you are able to pay for them. To top it up, you are prepared for anything that comes your way due to the fact that you have an emergency fund to cater for that.

7.   Less organizing required

When you buy fewer items then you have fewer things to clean, maintain and organize. This will give you an easy time and more room to engage in other activities.

8.   Debt free

We often get in to debts to be able to live the life we want and cater for unplanned emergencies. Since living frugally will help you to save up for emergencies and spend less, you will save money and will not have a reason to accumulate debts which is a great life free of worries. You will be able to use the money you have for other important projects and not be working full time to repay unending debts.

Questions to ask yourself to determine how frugal you are

LIVING FRUGALLY

There are many people who find themselves in serious financial situations and in worse cases they may not even be in a position to settle their debts and bills. These people may be failing in the way they spend their money in the sense that they are extremely frugal in some areas of their lives and spend unnecessarily in other respects. You may be wondering whether or not you are frugal enough and these are the questions you can ask yourself to help you determine that.

Do you choose generic items found at the store or are you into store brands?

It is common for many people to want things that are associated with the name brand of whatever they are buying. If this is the case then you are not frugal and you can go for the store brand because they are also good and cost less.

Do you consume tobacco, energy drinks, alcohol, soda or drugs?

You might not think twice about buying these drinks but if you make it a habit then you will spend needlessly and this is not being frugal. These are expensive yet they affect your health negatively in the long run. If you are frugal then you will be very careful about how you spend on these.

Do you use basic cable or extra satellite Channels and additional cable?

A frugal person can do with the basic cable but if you need all the additional things that you have to purchase or pay for monthly then you are not frugal.

How do you run your thermostat in accordance to the season?

You may not think of something as simple as the number of the thermostat but this can distinguish whether or not you are a frugal person. If you don't change it all year round then you are wasting a lot of money. When you alternate it in relation to the particular season you are in, you may not notice the change but it will manifest itself in your energy bill.

Do you eat out regularly?

If you are used to eating out regularly when with your coworkers then you are not frugal because this is expensive. Frugal people prefer to carry packed food from home and save money.

Do you pay for extra phone bill charges?

There are many extra charges that people who are not frugal pay for such as unlimited texts and data that are never used, call waiting charges and so on. If you finding yourself concerned with the type of bills you pay for and reduce them then you are frugal.

Are you spending extra on yourself, your spouse or child?

As we have mentioned earlier you might wonder why you are in a financial crisis when you think you are frugal but the reality is that you might be overspending on some areas and these are some of them. It is easy to give your spouse or child some money and not think about it but they do add up to your expenses. If you have this habit then you are not frugal.

How do you use your light bulbs?

Something as small as the type of light bulb you use can determine whether or not you are frugal. Efficient bulbs are what frugal people use and they don't leave their bulbs on when sleeping, out or if there is no one in the room.

Do you know about the foods that are in your cupboards or pantry?

There are many times that people leave foods inside their cupboards or pantry for such a long time that they forget about them and the food even goes bad. People who are frugal on the other hand buy the food they are able to consume and so you are frugal if you know the foods you have in your kitchen.

Are you used to driving to places where you can use public transport?

There are times when public transport can do when going some places in addition to being cheap. If you find yourself always driving even to such places then you are not frugal.

Chapter 9: A Brief Introduction Of Frugal Living

So, you have finally made a decision of frugal living. But before I tell you exactly how to apply some proven strategies and tips, let me explain you exactly what frugal living is. Many people often misunderstand the term "frugal living" and they think that it means living miserably to save every penny that you earn, but frugal living is not connected to misery. Frugal living is like a management of your expenses and budget. Every person has certain budget for the month and he must manage his budget uniformly to stay away from a high amount of debt. Frugal living doesn't mean that you should doom yourself to a life of deprivation and misery. It is about living smarter and spending on something that is more essential for you.

Frugal living is the best way to manage your budget so that you can do smarter money management. You can learn some techniques of frugal living to make better decisions of how and where to spend your money. You must ask yourself before buying anything expensive for yourself like – "Can I afford a new pair of shoes or are they really necessary right now?" When you ask yourself these questions, then you'll definitely know what you can afford, and more importantly what you cannot afford.

Before you apply the techniques of frugal living of this book in your life, my suggestion would be to make a positive mindset towards frugal living. There are many techniques to live frugal in your life, but I have seen many people who cannot continue applying these techniques because they don't set their minds to apply those techniques. Once you make a positive mindset, then I am sure that you will continue applying techniques of my book and thus live a happy and prosperous life. Today, many people send me e-mails and call me to say thanks for the strategies that I have shared in my book. They said that they never knew that their life will become so prosperous and beautiful after applying frugal living strategies of my book.

Find a Way to Save Few Bucks Everyday

You would be amazed to know that there are many ways to save few bucks every day. If you are obsessed to branded cloths and luxury shoes then try to improve your habit a bit. I have seen in many people that they wear branded clothes, but lack in self confidence. If you have a high level of self confidence in yourself, then I am sure that any casual dress would do the work that most branded clothes without self confidence won't be able to do. The most effective way to increase your self confidence is to shred little weight from your body and look fit and fine. I am sure that the amount you invest in the gym will make miraculous changes in your life as compared to the amount you spend on branded clothes and shoes. There are many other ways to save a little bit of amount everyday like you can rent DVD's if you love to watch movies instead of visiting multiplexes and throwing money on expensive food and drinks.

Use Debit Cards Instead of Credit Cards for Shopping

Credit cards have become a trend nowadays and every person uses them. Credit cards are good in some cases where you get a discount on your shopping. But addiction to credit cards is not beneficial. Many studies have proved that people tend to spend 50-60% more when they buy something through credit cards instead of other means of payment. There are many branded stores who just make you fool showing you fake offers of buy one get one and grab a huge amount of cash from your bank balance. I would suggest you to choose wisely and think twice before you see any attractive offers on the internet, TV, or newspaper about discounts. You also have to pay a huge interest on your bills of credit cards if you don't pay the bill within the turnaround time. So, use debit cards or some other means of payment whenever you go for shopping. Credit cards may be beneficial for making some purchase from E-commerce sites, because they provide you many offers and discounts.

Use Automatic Payment Options for Paying Your Monthly Bills

Your monthly bills are your major concern and you must pay them monthly to remain away from any kind of penalty. Use internet banking autopay method to pay your monthly bills automatically. This way you don't have to pay any penalty and you can manage your remaining savings for other purpose. Today, there are many online payment processor websites that should pay you discounts and offers for using their autopay system. Find a legit website that provides these facilities in your area and apply the autopay option for paying your bills.

Start an Automatic Savings Plan

After you learn how to save few bucks every day, your next step is to sign up for an automatic savings plan. The amount of your automatic savings would be exactly around 20% or more of your monthly income. This way you can really save big without worrying about your home budget. Many SIP investment plans are available today that needs only a few dollars of investment monthly and you don't need to be an investment geek to make the investments. SIP or Systematic investment plans have a benefit that an investment manager will do all the investing on your behalf and it is less risky than investing in share markets. You must apply for a long term investment plant like 15-25 year plan for best results. I myself have realized that SIP's are much better than saving your money in any fixed deposits or in the bank. They can provide you 20% interest per annum if you invest for long terms of about 15-25 years.

Make Future Plans and Use Envelop Method

You must make some future plans for your monthly investment. You have already done the automatic part of frugal living like autopay for your bills and automatic savings, but still you need some hard cash in your hands to spend on day to day living. Whenever you get your salary updated in your account, start making future plans for your money after putting essential money for your monthly budget. I would suggest you to make a list of what you want so that you can cross check the list in the next month. Now, take your list and see what is important that you need to buy, like you need new tyres for your car or you need to do some maintenance work for your home. Cross the unnecessary items and invest in what is that you need most at the time.

Make some envelops and put the amount inside them and name them, e.g. put enough money for your monthly grocery items in one envelop and name it. Make another envelope and put enough money for the things that you need urgent like your car's maintenance. This way you can really save your time and money to spend on unnecessary items.

Get Some Cash from Your Clutter

Banishing your clutter for some cash is a good way not only to make some space in your home, but also to earn some cash. I have seen many people that they are obsessed about their gifts, books, or clothing. They gather so many clothes, books, and gifts in their shelf that it almost looks very awful. You can banish your clutter and make your shelf look elegant and beautiful, thereby earning few bucks on your old items.

You can find many items in your garage and shelf that you can sell for a few bucks at a consignment store or on eBay. Certain items like vintage clothing can bring higher prices on auctions at eBay, than at consignment as a result of competitive bidding. The best way to sell your items on eBay is to compare the price of other items and place your item at a certain lower price, if you want to accelerate the process of selling. The most effective way to sell on eBay is to provide lots of information about the item you are selling.

Most people who buy from eBay want to feel comfortable about the quality and authenticity of the item, or they won't buy your item. Take some HD images from different angles and provide a brief description about the brand, quality, and date of the item you purchased.

Now, if you have many books that are making your shelf look awful and termites are feeding on them, then I would suggest selling them on Amazon. Amazon is the best site to sell your old books since Amazon list your books with other regular priced item and if you sell your book at lower price, then you have more chances to sell your book. This allows savvy customers to compare the prices and see who is offering the best deals.

Finally, the last option to banish your clutter is to donate them. Donating something is not only the best option for doing some charity, but it also has some tax benefits. Ask your accountant about the tax benefits of donating and contact an NGO near you who is willing to provide you a receipt of your donations of the exact amount of your items.

Getting rid of your clutter doesn't only make your home look good, but it has also some positive effect on your brain. Many studies have proved that a person living in cluttered home has more behavioural issues as compared to the person who banish his clutter often. People can feel some kind of relief from their inner self when they banish their clutter and live a beautiful life.

Chapter 10: How to Get Started with

Living Frugally

Many people are choosing to live a frugal lifestyle, as I have said before. Let's look at a few reasons you should be living frugal.

Many people have experienced job losses in recent times. Businesses and large corporations are closing down many of their offices, leaving thousands to thousands without jobs or income. One who loses their job is forced to live frugally. They may find that they can find another job, and that it allows them to keep the money they've worked so hard for.

Debt Relief - Everyone has debt in some way or another. This could be educational debt, loan debts, medical debts, credit card debts, and so on. We all know that debt can begin small, but in a matter of minutes can quickly grow into a large amount of debt. Many people's first instinct is to go to the nearest loan officer to get yet another debt. This will only result in them having to pay off existing debt. This is a terrible idea. It doesn't get rid of debt and only adds to your worries. Start living a frugal lifestyle, and you will see your debt decrease until it is gone.

People are transforming to a frugal lifestyle because of retirement. Many companies do not offer retirement plans. If you are self-employed, you will need to create your own retirement plan. You can make your life more frugal and save money for your retirement. People don't often think about a retirement plan when they are young. They spend every penny on living expenses, entertainment, and other cash-squandering activities, without thinking about how they will survive when they get older and become unable to work.

It's easy to do, and people don't need the extra money to put together a retirement plan. Then, when they reach retirement age, they realize they cannot retire as they don't have enough funds. However, living frugally can help you create your own retirement plan.

Living frugally is also popular for those with low incomes or little to no pay rises. Another reason people have to live cheaply is because they are forced to. Living a frugal life can help people relieve stress. They won't have to spend as much on their daily expenses, but they will still be able to live a full and happy life. Low income families can now live frugally, which many consider a growing trend.

These are only a few reasons people are choosing to live a frugal life. But there are many other reasons. You are probably interested in how your family can live a more frugal lifestyle. Let's start by describing a few things that you can do to prepare you and your family for your "frugal" lifestyle.

You must first get your family on the same page. Your ability to get your family on the same page about frugal living is crucial. This doesn't mean that you have to view it as something that your family must live with. Instead, make sure that your family sees the positive changes.

It is not easy for many people to get their children to be frugal. When it comes to how and in what amount the family's income should be distributed, everyone needs to agree. Limits will be needed, not like a prison, but ones that are manageable and reduce the amount of money spent each day.

Your family should be able to see the benefits of living a frugal lifestyle. They need to understand how they can still enjoy life and not spend hundreds of dollars. Your main goal is to get your family to agree and live a frugal life.

Your family can set a goal with a reward at the end. You could also offer your family a reward for their efforts by taking a vacation after a year of frugal living. You will probably do your vacationing "frugally," but this is a great incentive for you to live the fugal lifestyle.

Many families discover that even though their spending habits and lifestyle have changed, they still manage to acquire the "nice" things they want. They also enjoy the enjoyment and entertainment of life while still being able to do the "frugal" things. You can start living "frugally" once you have your family on the same page and you work together to make it possible.

Chapter 11: The Importance Of Budgeting

For Frugal Living

It is most important, when one decides to stick to living a frugal lifestyle, to seriously consider budgeting when it comes to ensuring that we really end up living well within our means. So why is budgeting really all that important? Do we really need a formalized system like the same to ensure that we do not end up exceeding the limits we have set for ourselves where it comes to spending money? Let's take a look at just why budgeting is so important for us where it comes to frugal living.

• It gives you control over your money. Where it comes to the process of spending your money, you really want to be in that driver's seat where it comes to spending the same rather than having the money in the bank dictate how much you ultimately end up spending. It helps you to plan sufficiently for the future to come and make important decisions like cutting

96

back on certain daily costs so that you can save up for a greater pleasure like say, taking your family on that vacation that you have been planning for so long. It helps you make your own individual choices where it comes to spending and saving your money, and makes sure that you do not end up being controlled by that money in the end, with little choice as to what you can do with it simply because there are far too limited funds in the bank because of your lack of planning.

• It helps maintain that sense of focus on your money goals. You will find that when you indulge in the process of sensible budgeting, you will not find the need to splurge on things that you don't need, in a conscious attempt to reach the financial goals you have outlined for yourself. Thus it will be a most plausible way to ensure that you make those ends meet, when you are in the process of working with very limited resources.

• You get to know what is happening with your money. Through the process of budgeting, you get to know exactly how much money is coming, how fast it is going and exactly where it is going, as well. It makes sure that you are able to understand exactly what it is you can afford and how you can take those vital steps towards lowering your debt. It also helps you to take advantage of those important buying and investing opportunities, that can make a good deal of difference to your money situation in the time to come. It helps to show you how you can allocate those funds of yours and how the money is working for you, as well, thereby giving you a good deal of understanding of your money, something that is essential if you need to be able to manage it well.

• It helps to organize your savings and spending. When you budget, you know which expenditure of yours falls into which specific category. This can help you tweak the same so that you are able to manage your money better. It also helps you organize those bills, receipts and financial statements, so that when they are needed for tax time and creditor questions, a lot of time and effort is saved in the process of procuring them.

• It helps you to save for both unexpected as well as expected costs. You will find that when an emergency strikes, it does so without warning and that is why it is all the more essential to budget in order to make sure that you are able to meet those unexpected costs that might arise in the case of an emergency.

• It enables you to share that responsibility of spending money with others. It is really most effective to employ budgeting if you are married or living with a partner, as it allows your partner to work alongside you in working through that all important process of budgeting. This can be a really good thing for you because it means that the process of learning to manage that money of yours becomes all the more transparent where it comes to your partner, and this means that a lot of that unnecessary conflict that might otherwise crop up, is done away with altogether. By working on the budget alongside you, your partner is also imbibed with a strong sense of responsibility where it comes to spending your money together and that only leads to a healthier relationship, as an outcome of the same. It also means that you are no longer the only person who will be held accountable in the end, where it comes to your financial situation.

• You can see those 'money problems' in advance. Through the process of budgeting you will find that you are able to pinpoint those serious money problems well in advance so that you can take care of them well in advance and letting things get blown out of proportion.

• It helps you determine the level of debt you can take on. It helps you paint a most realistic picture of the debt that you can take on and whether it is really worth it to take on the same.

• It helps to eliminate those additional costs. There are several additional costs that might be incurred by you, that can be done away completely through the process of budgeting. These are things like late fees, penalties and interests which can be identified well in advance and hence these small savings of yours that you make will add up considerably over time and you will find that you have all the more money accrued as a result of the same, which will really come as a sort of most welcome bonus for you!

• It helps you work towards that retirement fund of yours. It is only through the process of astute budgeting that you will find out juts how exactly you can contribute to retirement funds that will enable you to amass a large sum of money that will be extremely beneficial in ensuring that you live a happy life in the years that follow your retirement. Simply saving money is not enough; there must be specific investments that are made in things like the IRA and 401(k) that will help you effectively achieve your goals of making that retirement fund of yours fatter than you could ever imagine it would be.

• It helps you to make those all-important 'changes'. At times you will find that certain costs rise, and if you ever found yourself wondering in the past as to how you would make those costs meet, you will find that budgeting will make this process a lot simpler for you, by enabling you to pinpoint exactly where that extra money is going to come from.

• It helps you 'cut back'. Just like you will find that you can 'cut back' somewhere in order to meet a cost like the one discussed in the point above, you will find that there are several other places where you can 'cut back', in the process of working on that budget of yours. You will be able to see that there are plenty of areas where you can do the same, in order to effectively reduce those outgoings of yours and consequently end up with a lot more money in the process.

• It helps you to set your priorities. When you actually get down to setting a budget, you come to realize that there are a certain things that are really more important to you than others, things that would have really gone unnoticed had you not taken the time to actually sit down to work on that budgeting process of yours. You will find that there are things like sending your child to a good school, that are far more important than planning that expensive trip to Europe every year for a few years down the road. The truth is, you really can't understand the costs that are involved in the future until you make a conscious attempt to put them down on paper. This makes you come face to face with the important need to make very real compromises in order to meet the priorities that really rank much higher than others in the grand scheme of things.

• It helps you to reach your goals faster. Like we have already discussed, budgeting helps you reach those financial goals that you have set for yourself with a far greater degree of certainty, but the thing to remember here is that you might even end up reaching those goals much faster than you would have envisioned, through the same process. This in turn means that you are far more capable to exceed the very goals that you have set for yourself, and you will find out that you will really end up laughing your way to the bank, in the process.

• It creates that all-important 'financial margin'. When you set that budget of yours, you will find yourself living within the budget that you have stipulated for every month. In the process of doing so, you will find that you will actually try to live well within that budget, to the point where there is some sum of money that is saved at the end. This sum of money is known as the 'financial margin' and it is most helpful as it can be used in order to meet other financial goals of yours that would have otherwise never been realized, if you hadn't kept a check on your spending through the process of budgeting.

• It helps to reduce stress on a consistent basis. One need not make a guess where it comes to determining whether that overseas vacation that one has planned will be affordable or not; through the process of budgeting one will find that at every step of the way, the unnecessary stress that comes along with not knowing if one can realize their goals or not, is eliminated as it paints a most realistic picture of just how much money is needed where, and how one can go about in actually making it happen!

• It serves as a 'living' roadmap to your plan. The thing one must understand in the case of a budget, is the fact that it is really a 'living document' and that there are times when things will occur unexpectedly, things that make you go out of sync with that original budgeting plan of yours. This need not serve as a source of worry for you at all, because it only means that you know every step of the way, where every single dollar of yours is being spent and that any changes in the plan that might arise when certain events occur, can be taken care of so as to realign yourself with the original 'route' that you have set for yourself in that financial budget of yours.

• It helps you make 'rational choices' where it comes to spending your money. Through the process of budgeting, you are no longer privy to the unwanted 'emotional spending' that is usually rampant in most big 'spenders' out there, but it also helps in making good solid choices in what you really 'do' need to invest in. This is because once you have gotten into the habit of budgeting you will find that you have an increased value for money and that you will come to see it more and more as a viable 'tool' that is to be used in building the life of your dreams. When you make the right choices you will find that your life will expand into avenues that you had once never quite imagined, paving the way for a completely different 'life' in the process!

Chapter 12: Entertainment

Enjoy watching the latest movies? The prices at the local theater are astounding. I checked out theaters charging absolutely ridiculously expensive prices for admission. This is an enormous expense for a family of four, if you add in popcorn, drinks, and parking fees. If you really must attend the theater or movie, consider attending the matinee. Matinee prices are lower. Bring your own microwaved popcorn and sneak your own soda and snacks into the theater. Food prices for those snacks in the movie theater are to the extreme. Go online and check for movie tickets offered at discount prices. Some theaters offer free tickets to movie goers for special movie events. Check for them frequently.

Watch Free Movies Online – It's true. Perhaps, you will not see the latest blockbusters for free, but there are literally thousands of films to view for free on sites like Hulu, YouTube, and Crackle.

All that is required is a fast Internet connection, browser, and computer. For a few dollars per month (about eight bucks) join Netflix and stream the latest blockbuster movies straight to your television or computer. This is a really good option. Certainly cheaper than spending hundreds at a movie theater per month.

Local Library – Do you have a library card? Local libraries are offering good family friendly entertainment movies for free. Check out your local library for more information.

Online Resources -Check Amazon.com, eBay, and DVD swap sites for cool deals on used DVD Movies. Purchase classics to the latest blockbuster movies. The savings are amazing on those sites. The DVD swap site will allow people who join the site to swap their DVD Movies with others. Joining the sites is free. Usually there is a charge to mail the DVD's. Still, it is a great way to save on entertainment.

Swap DVD Movies with your friends and family. Keep the movies rotating through the family until everyone has viewed them. Throw special movie parties rather than going to the movies every weekend. Pop your own popcorn, serve drinks and snacks to the guest. Make it a fun and entertaining event. Create a theater vibe by filling the viewing room with movie posters and pictures.

Check out the local entertainment options at city events, cultural events, local universities or colleges. These are great resources for family friendly entertainment.

Visit your local bookstore. Read books and magazines for free. Bookstores like Barnes & Noble allow their customers to browse through the magazine racks and book shelves. Many take the books and magazines to browse through or read for hours and then return them to the shelves or rack.

Game On – Start a game night with friends and family. Dust off the scrabble or monopoly board and have some good old fashion fun playing those classic games.

Book Club – Organize a book club with a few friends. Check the books out of the library to save money. Meet every week to discuss the book. This is a fun and entertaining way to spend time with friends.

PC Games – Why spend hundreds on games for your computer. There are millions of games that are available for free download online. Check out sites like CNet's downloads.com for good games that you instantly download and play for free. Remember, it is not always about spending money on the hottest games, but simply having fun.

Enjoy the View – Get outside and walk around your neighborhood parks and recreation centers. Enjoy the fresh air, nature, and life around you. Go for a bike ride on bike trails in the park or go for a fun hike through the park. Pack a lunch and make it a fun and entertaining event with the family.

Get Recreational. Recreational centers are fun places to meet others and share fun time. Visit the recreational centers in your community in summer that have pools. Spend hot summer days swimming and having a blast. Some recreational centers also offer summer camps, free games, and special movie nights for families.

Play Games. The family that plays together stays together. Get the family together and play games. Toss the ball around, shoot some hoops, toss the football, race, bike, roller blade, jog, skateboard. You will burn some calories and have lots of fun

Hobbies. Start a website concerning your hobby. Or simply start blogging about your life and sharing pictures and stories. Open an account at Google's Blogger for free.

Coupons Entertainment. Purchase discount entertainment coupon books which cost less than thirty bucks. These coupon books offer enormous discounts at local restaurants, hotels, theaters, shops, and a variety of other places.

Chapter 13: Frugalism In The Kitchen

One of the greatest leaks in the budget occurs in the kitchen. Improper meal planning and shopping can blow your entire budget quickly. Here are some great tips to save you money in the kitchen and get you closer to your goal of being an awesome frugalista.

• Plan your meal — This has got to be the most important of all the tips. Sit down each week and plan your meals, including what you will pack for lunches. Write it down to the very last detail and post it on the fridge. Try to plan meals that incorporate many of the same ingredients. Watch your portion sizes. So much waste goes into the trash from cooking too much. If there are leftovers, freeze them and make it a meal for another day.

• Simplify — Make simple meals. Soups and casseroles make for fabulous and satisfying meals with few ingredients. Look for "one pot" recipes. Instead of buying breads and cakes, learn to bake. A bowl of simple soup and a piece of flatbread made with just flour, salt, and water is a delicious winter supper. In the summer, make a meal of roasted corn and potatoes. A vegetarian lifestyle is always a good option for cutting expenses in the kitchen.

•	Do batch cooking — Cook meals ahead of time and freeze them. This will save time and conserve energy. For instance, if you are making a veggie lasagna with vegetables from your own garden, why not make two at the same time? Have one for supper and freeze the other. Now, you have an already prepared meal that you will only have to heat up.

•	Make your own snacks — Clip recipes from magazines or copy them from cookbooks. A great money saver is learning how to create your own delicious and healthy snacks instead of buying them. Oats, granola, raisins, and popcorn are great go-to foods when you are looking for something in between meals.

Popcorn itself can be flavored in many different ways.

• Be a smart shopper — Take the time to make a list before you head out to the grocery store. By planning your meals down to the last ingredient, you will know exactly what to buy. Then stick to the list. Compare brands and consult your coupons. Many times you will find products with the exact same ingredients for a lot less than what you normally buy. Off-brand products that don't pay for expensive advertising is a good place to start. Generic drugs and medicines are always a great choice. Also, get to know your grocery store's layout so you don't spend too much time roaming the aisles. Get in and get out. More importantly, never shop on an empty stomach.

• Preserve your goods — Learning to can and preserve food is a great way to save money and have healthy, ready-to-eat snacks and sides on hand. Canning does require some skill, but surely you can find some books about it in the library. If not, use the library's computers to watch some videos and take notes. Jams, jellies, and even peanut butter can be made right in your own kitchen. Imagine a peanut butter and jelly sandwich on your own homemade flatbread. Kids will love it.

• Bulk up — Buy your basic pantry items in bulk and portion them out when you get home. You want to buy ingredients that will turn into meals, not ready-to-eat snacks. Stay away from boxed or frozen meals. Keep around things like flour, canned or frozen vegetables, rice, tomato sauces and paste, beans, and oil, and invest in spices. This will ensure you always have something on hand to make a meal (if you haven't pre-planned) and won't be running out for takeout or ordering pizza.

• Stock up on baking soda and vinegar — There are many simple products found in every kitchen that have several amazing uses. Vinegar, for one, works wonders not only as a delicious salad dressing, but it can also be used for cleaning windows, unclogging drains, deodorizing, and cutting grease. Baking soda is another product that has endless uses. Combining a little baking soda and hydrogen peroxide make for a potent toothpaste at a fraction of the cost. Research at the library or online. You will be amazed by what you'll find.

Chapter 14: A Fresh Start

Before you ever even think about using frugal living to get yourself out of debt, you need to make sure you are in the right frame of mind. It's not a temporary solution. If you reduce your spending now, then go back to spending beyond your means once you've eliminated your debt, you'll probably end up back in debt, and find yourself facing the same situation you were in before.

You also have to look at the changes that you are making and think of it as starting fresh. Yes, you will need to make some sacrifices now, but think about all the benefits you'll reap from it. Think of how amazing it will feel to bring home a paycheck that doesn't all go on paying off your debts? Imagine what life will be like when you have no car payment, no credit card debt, or even no mortgage payment every month? Think of all the great things your income can do for you when it belongs JUST to you.

Fight the fear, find financial freedom

You may be putting off making the changes necessary to get out of debt because they feel scary and like too much work, but think about how you feel every time you have to pay a credit card bill or loan payment. Think about how you feel when the week lasts longer than your paycheck, and you can't quite figure out which bill to pay first and which to let run overdue. Those feelings of anxiety over not having enough money are way worse than any minor discomforts you'll feel when you begin living frugally.

For some people, It can help to make a list of the things that they'd like to have or achieve once they are debt-free. List any financial price attached to these things, then look at one small habit or regular purchase that you could sacrifice to save for those things.

• Could you give up that pricey gourmet coffee from the coffee shop, or reduce the number of times you buy one each week?

• Could you take a lunch to work every day instead of eating fast food?

• Could you stop smoking, or cut back, to help save for your dream purchase? (This would save you money in health costs, too!)

There are probably dozens of small ways you could reduce your spending every week to put money towards getting out of debt or saving for a dream purchase. Many of these expenses seem so small that you might be tempted to think they don't make a big difference, but they do. If you drink five-$5 coffees every week, over the course of a year that equals $1300.

If you make a few small sacrifices every week, you probably won't miss the things you give up that much. Just make sure you replace them with free or low-cost alternatives, and you won't even feel deprived. For example, make yourself a cup of flavored coffee at home instead of buying from the coffee shop, cook tasty meals to take to work, etc. Most little luxuries have a cheaper or free alternative if you are willing to look for them.

Keeping a positive outlook is crucial to successful frugal living. If you go around telling yourself that you're being deprived, you'll just give into self-pity and fall off the wagon, slipping into the same bad habits that got you into debt in the first place. Staying positive means finding ways to appreciate the things you have when you are choosing to have less, and it means reminding yourself that the outcome is worth any temporary discomfort you feel that you might be experiencing. In other words, the struggle won't last forever, and if you stick with it, frugal living could be the most rewarding way to live your life because you will look forward to a great financial future.

Learning to say goodbye to old spending habits may be difficult, but it's not impossible, and it signifies the beginning of a new start to your finances. Once you can get past the feelings of 'woe is me,' you'll probably start to realize how lucky you are. After all, people in third world countries aren't complaining about having to give up a latte so they can afford to retire comfortably, so it may help to keep your 'sacrifices' in perspective.

And whenever you're tempted to feel jealous of your friends and family who are still living the high life, eating out every other night and spending way more money than you, just remember that you only see a tiny piece of their overall picture. They may have once been where you are now, but made their own sacrifices and are now enjoying the fruits of their efforts.

Or, they could be heading down the rabbit hole you just started clawing your way out of, financing their lifestyle with credit cards that will have to be paid off sooner or later. Who knows, maybe they'll see the changes that you are making in your life and commit to making some of their own. You could be the catalyst that helps others get their financial lives back on track, and that is hugely satisfying and very cool.

Squash the jealous feelings, kick the fears and doubts to the curb, and set your mind on success. A clean-slate state of mind will help you laser in on achieving your financial goals and meet them head on, so you can plan an awesome future.

Chapter 15: How to Shop Frugally

You can start to transform your lifestyle by changing how you shop. You have many options to make your shopping more efficient and save money. These are some tips and ideas to help you make the transition to a more frugal shopping style.

Plan your Shopping Trip - Many frugal families find that one shopping trip per week reduces their living expenses and also lowers gas costs. A list can be kept on your refrigerator so that family members can note the "necessary". Next, take a look at your list and ensure that you have everything you need for the week. Plan your route to each of the places you'll be shopping.

This will reduce the fuel required to travel to each destination. Online shopping can help you save gas. This is a popular choice for many people. You can also find better deals online and get coupons.

Use Coupons as Much as Possible - Coupons can help you save hundreds each week on both common household products and food products. Most weeks, your weekly newspaper will include a set coupon that you can print out and use on your next shopping trip. Coupons can make a huge difference in how much you save, which will translate into more money at the end.

Online printable coupons can be found at sites like www.coupons.com. You can also find coupons for top-brand products online that will help you save money on your next shopping trip. Coupons can be a great way for you to live a frugal lifestyle. They should be used every time you shop for groceries and retail items.

Wholesale Membership Clubs - These clubs allow you to buy both retail and grocery items in bulk. This saves you both time and money. Sam's Club, a wholesale membership club, is a great way for you to save money on everyday products that can be bought in bulk at a lower price than what you would pay individually. While you will need to pay a modest membership fee, you can also get discounts on store items, gas, tires and many other benefits. Membership clubs offer a great way for people to save money monthly. Many people have a spare freezer or garage that they can use to store frozen food. This is a great way of buying items in bulk and then using them throughout the month. This method of shopping "frugally" will save you a lot.

Use Secondhand Stores to your Advantage - People are increasingly flocking to thrift shops for household and clothing items. Many secondhand thrift shops not only sell items that have been used before, but also stock items from other retail stores that have closed down after a certain season. Your retail stores may have excess inventory and will not be able to sell all of their stock at the end of the season. Secondhand shops will sell these items at a very low rate. Many times, secondhand thrift shops will stock items that have never been worn or used. Most of these items still have their price tags attached. You can often find name-brand products at a fraction of retail price.

Retail sellers can also sell furniture outlets and high-end furniture stores. If an item is deemed "old", and there are still many of the same items in stock, they will also sell it to secondhand thrift shops at a very low price. Many people avoid thrift shops because they fear being considered lower class. This is where my thoughts are very honest. "How can people know where you bought the clothing or brand name items if you don't tell them?" Many of your most coveted brands and names are available in secondhand thrift shops and are in great to excellent condition. You can save a lot of money by buying at low prices instead of spending the same amount elsewhere for the exact brands and products.

Generic vs. name brand items - Generic is the best way to save money and live cheaply. This is a great way to save money and live more comfortably on household goods and food products. Many top retailers are now creating their own brands for your favorite products at a fraction of what it costs to buy the same brand items. These retailers have created a new trend by offering the same quality products that their competitors. Generic brand products can save you money! Make sure to shop generic for all your household items and food products.

Comparative Shopping is a great way to find the best price for items you use every day, weekly or monthly. You might find one item cheaper in one location than the other, but it could be the same thing the next week. You should always be on the lookout for bargains when you shop for items you use often.

Online Shopping - You can shop for the exact same products online as you would in stores, and you can do it all from your home. You can shop online for many products at a fraction of the cost you'd find in a local grocery store or retail store. Additionally, you can also find coupons and codes that will help you save even further!

While shipping costs can be expensive in certain cases, you may still get free shipping if you spend a certain amount on their site. You can save a lot of money by getting the discounted rate and also saving on shipping costs. This is the best deal! This is a great way to live for your family and you'll find more money at the end.

Avoid impulse purchases - Last but not least, it is important to avoid impulse buying at all costs. Many people will wander the aisles of grocers or retail stores looking for something they "have to have". I know because I have been there. Mind control is a key part of your game. It is important to be able tell yourself "No!" and that this item is not within your budget or a "necessity", then you can simply walk away.

There will be times when you don't have enough money to buy a large item. This isn't an expensive item, but it is a nice treat. When shopping, keep in mind your goals and be frugal. Once you have been living a "frugal" lifestyle for a while, impulse purchases will be a thing of the past. Keep in mind that your lifestyle is now cheaper so you can live better later.

You don't need to make shopping for groceries and household essentials a nightmare. These tips and suggestions can help you save money on your future, as well as keep more money in your pockets. These strategies will make a big difference in your shopping experience and the savings you can make for your family.

Chapter 16: The Debt -Free Plan

The Debt-Free Plan is extremely simple and easy to implement. All that it takes is two stages.

Stage One

Never use consumer credit. Never use charge cards if you can't pay the balance off in full when the bill comes. If you can't pay cash for it, you don't need it. Cut up your charge cards and throw them all away. (I rarely pay cash, rather I use an American Express Card which I pay off in full each month and a No-Fee Visa card that I use at places that do not take American Express. However, I always pay the Visa card off in full each month. I never carry a balance. These cards give me frequent flyer miles and a record for tax purposes. So while I rarely use actual cash, I am in essence using the modern version of cash). If you are in debt and unwilling to destroy your charge cards then you are doomed. You are nothing more than a Level One Investor. You must end the cycle now! Go ahead and take your charge cards out and put them in front of you. Think about all the problems they have caused you. Think about the debt. The monthly payments. The pain. The slavery. The bondage. Now cut them up.

Stage Two

Stage Two is to add 10% to your minimum payments. For example, if your monthly payments total to $2,000. You would pay $2,200 (an increase of 10%). However, you are not going to just add 10% to each bill. Rather, you are going to strategically place the extra 10% on the bill we can eliminate the fastest. Continue doing this based on the budget you had allocated and see some fascinating things happening before your eyes. And the end of the change that is a turn around you will start feeling you did it all by yourself.

What to get rid of and what to keep with you

Get rid of the high interest loans and the credit card debts you have. Start with the debt that has the lowest balance and the highest interest rate on it. And change this with smaller bills that you can pay off real fast. Getting rid of the highest interest rate first will save you the most money in a long run. It can be disheartening, so irregular between the bigger and smaller bills will help you feel like you are getting to some point. The solution is to quickly reduce these debts and stick to your plan.

Track every dollar you spend

You know how much you get in, but do you know where all that is going? One of the initial steps in preparing your budget is tracking your expenditure. Gather all of your receipts for the month and detach them into three categories: fixed, variable and supplementary expenses. You may be amazed at how much you are spending on flexible expenses and needless items. Use this info to free up some of your money so you can easily add to your emergency or rainy day fund.

Take steps to reduce flexible expenses.

Flexible expenses, such as utility bills, groceries and money spent on clothes are some of the simple expenses to cut back on. Call your mobile phone company and exchange a better rate, use coupons for your monthly groceries, buy in large (in bulk if possible) and shop for clothing at discounted shops.

You can take extra steps to save money on food items by: planning your food intake ahead of time, making a priority list and sticking to it, carrying up on sale items and having your lunch while you are at work.

Chapter 17: How To Make A Budget

Now that we have seen the importance of having a budget through all the possible benefits that we have gleaned in the last chapter, it's time to taker a look and see just how we can actually set to work on creating that budget of ours. Let's take a look at all the steps that we need to undertake, where it comes to creating that perfect budget of ours.

Step One: Find out the amount of money you have

You really need to know exactly how much you are worth, and this entails finding out how much money lies in each account of yours, be it savings, investments or checking. You also need to know the interest rates and expenses of each of these accounts.

Step Two: Determine how much money you make

Of , this is a no-brainer if it comes to you being on a salary, but if you are receiving income on a not so regular basis, you might want to average out the last six to twelve months of recurring income and use the figure that you get, in order to arrive at the average monthly income. If you want to be ultra conservative in your approach, you might consider using the lowest monthly income that you have accrued in the last one year, as your average monthly income that will be used for the budgeting process that is to follow.

Step Three: Find out how much money you owe

This is the stage where you determine your monthly recurring debt payments. This is when you have to calculate the total amount owed on each dent account, as well as the minimum monthly payment. This includes car loans, student loans, credit card debt, mortgages and all the other debt that your family pays on a monthly basis.

Step Four: Determine your net worth

Once you have an idea s to the amount of money you have and the amount you owe, it is most easy to determine your net worth. All you have to do is subtract what you owe from what you have. Don't be surprised if you have a negative net worth; a lot of people out there who have taken on a lot of debt find themselves in a position like this, and therefore it is all the more essential for going in for that process of budgeting which will serve to ensure that you get out of that high interest debt situation far sooner than you otherwise would.

Step Five: Find out your average recurring monthly expenses

This is the most important component of that budget and is often the hardest part. The best way to determine your expenses for a month is to make a list of your household expenses for one month. You have to keep any bills and receipts that arise in the period of one particular month and segregate them into the appropriate categories. These categories will fall into the likes of things like car/entertainment/food, etc.

Step Six: Enter all the information into a database

Now that you have all the monthly expenses segregated, it is time that you get them formally entered into a database. All you need is a good tried and tested program like Microsoft Excel and you are good to go. You might even wish to use certain online budgeting tools for the same, but the former works juts as well. Once you have all this information entered, glancing at the bottom line will give you an idea of juts how much you are overspending, if you are overspending in the very first place, that is.

Step Seven: Make the necessary adjustments

Once you have seen that bottom line and understood that you have really been 'overspending', you will have to make all the necessary 'tweaks' in order to cut back on certain areas where you really might be spending far more than required, in order to ensure that that bottom line remains well under control and you do not end up overspending way too much. You have to make sure that you make these 'adjustments' in accordance with the realities that surround you; you will find that food prices increase and gas prices rise as a result of inflation and thus have to act accordingly. At the same time you might have gotten a raise at work, which might make it even easier to accommodate certain 'excesses' into that budget of yours. Make sure that you tweak that budget most 'realistically', in order to arrive at the best possible results.

Step Eight: Make those 'savings' a monthly recurring expense

You have to treat that 'savings' account of yours as a monthly recurring expense of yours and not something that is filled with what you have left over at the end of the month. For this reason you must ensure that you keep aside a provision for a certain amount of money that 'has' to go into that savings account of yours, whatever it might be, every single month. That will ensure that you never end up failing to add to that savings fund of yours, which should really be built up most consistently over time in order to ensure that you are left with a sufficient amount of money in it at the end.

Step Nine: Track that budget

What you need to understand, is that that budget of yours is 'living', like we have already touched upon in this book and that one needs to constantly monitor it and see that we are well on the path to financial success by being constantly on the path that we have defined for ourselves while setting it. All it takes, really, is to sit over that budget for just an hour or so every week, and that will ensure that you will be constantly comforted with the fact that you are indeed making a great deal of progress where it comes to achieving both your short and long term financial goals.

Chapter 18: Extra Income

If you're looking to increase your savings and reduce your debt, saving money is a great place to start. But don't forget about earning extra money.

We already talked about selling the things you don't need. But you can also make money in other ways. The internet is a great tool for freelancers. There are a number of sites that help freelancers find clients and that allow you to work from home in your spare time. Also, for some quick, relatively simple ways to make money, take a look at Amazon Mechanical Turk. That is a program that allows you to engage in short tasks (taking surveys, for example) and it pays you a small amount for each one you complete. It won't make you rich, but it'll put a few extra dollars in your pocket.

If you like to write, you should also consider writing ebooks to sell here on Amazon. Not only can you make extra money, but you will keep your mind sharp and hopefully enjoy yourself in the process.

You don't have to work multiple jobs just to save money. And if you aren't interested in seeking more work to earn income, then that's ok. But if you're able to do something you like while also getting paid for it, why not do it?

Chapter 19: Be thrifty: Buy secondhand stuff

You shouldn't be afraid of shopping at consignment shops, thrift stores, yard sales, and flea markets. People who have a lot of money are more likely to avoid thrift shops, thinking they are too rich to purchase and reuse second-hand goods. Thrift stores are great places to find gently used items, unless you have enough money to not need them.

This tip is not necessary if you are averse to the idea of thrift shopping. This means that I and other people who are in the know will get more deals. You may miss out on rare books, antiques, and designer clothes at a fraction the price they would cost elsewhere.

These are just a handful of the great smoking deals I found in local thrift shops over the past year.

* 5 books for $1.00 This was a special deal for one day only and included all books in the store. This deal included hardcover and children's books.

* An antique tea set for $25. The same set was selling on Ebay for $300 when I returned home.

* Brand-name designer clothing starting at $1.

For $2, I can get ink cartridges for my printer. I usually pay $25 for each cartridge.

* A clock radio starting at $1.25

For $45., get a solid oak kitchen table with chairs.

To get the best deals, keep an eye out for sales at your local thrift shops. My thrift shops offer discount days that allow you to get all the items of a particular type at a discount. Half off books for a day. All shirts will go for a dollar the next day. All pants will be two dollars the day after. Every day they have something new and great deals.

Find out the best time to shop at your favorite shops. Thrift shops replenish their stock every day. I check my favorite thrift stores at least once per week to find new items. The early bird wins when it comes to yard sales and flea markets. To score the best deals, be there as soon as you can.

Do not be afraid to disagree. Although thrift shops are unlikely to lower prices, you can still get them reduced at flea markets, consignment stores and yard sales. You can start with a low price and then work your way up. It's possible to be surprised at how willing people are to lower their asking prices.

Appliances

Appliances can be bought at great prices if you look out for signs of misuse or abuse. An appliance that is in poor condition will likely be at the end its useful life. You should look out for cracks, chips, frayed cords, and rust.

Always ask to test an appliance. It's easy to tell if a salesperson won't allow you to test it. You might be purchasing a high-priced paperweight if they refuse to let you test it. Reputable second-hand shops will always let you plug in an item to check if it works. They have likely tried it before putting it on the shelves, and they are happy to let you test it.

Books

Books can be purchased for as low as 10 percent of the cover price. For a few books, I have found hardcover books on sale for as low as $30 at my local thrift shop.

My daughter is a prolific reader and I wouldn't mind spending full retail to buy her books. I'm happy to buy her books for a few dollars, especially if I can sell them at a garage sales for the same price.

You can make a lot of money selling rare books online or at thrift shops if you are knowledgeable about the subject. A few people make a decent living by going thrift store to thrift shop looking for rare books that they can sell. They might buy a book for just a dollar, then sell it for fifty dollars or more.

Clothing

Thrift stores offer some of the most affordable clothing deals. You can find shirts starting at a dollar apiece, sweaters starting at $3 per piece, pants starting at $3-4, and coats between $5-10 at thrift stores. We start shopping for clothes a month in advance, whether it's for ourselves or the kids. Then we go to all the local thrift shops.

Start early when shopping for school clothes or seasonal clothing. This will allow you to be ahead of the rest and find the best deals. You may find clothes with tags or clothes that have been worn only once or twice.

These are some things that will make shopping for clothes easier. Before you buy clothing, make sure that all buttons and zippers are working properly. Make sure you check the clothing for any stains, tears or rips.

Make sure you check the return policy for clothing that you purchase. If you don't like your Christmas cardigan, you may not be allowed to return it. Many thrift shops have fitting rooms where you can try on any item that isn't quite right.

It's easy to save money on clothes. My family's annual clothing budget has been cut by several hundred dollars by shopping mostly at thrift shops.

Furniture

You might get more furniture than you expected when you buy it. I will not buy fabric that may be contaminated with fleas or bed-bugs. I avoid couches, recliners, and mattresses that might be crawling with bugs.

Before you buy any fabric furniture or mattresses, make sure to inspect it carefully before paying the money. You should look out for signs of infestation such as eggs or bugs tucked between cushions and seams. Once they have entered your home, you can quickly get rid of them.

I don't have any reservations about buying wood furniture at a thrift shop and have found some great deals. Apart from the solid oak table, I also purchased two bookcases as well as an entertainment center at a fraction of the cost of a new bookcase.

Toys

You can find many toys in thrift shops for children who are young. Children don't care if a toy is used, and neither should you. My kids get most of their toys from the thrift store, with the exception of a few gifts for Christmas and birthdays.

Before you give the toys to your children, clean them and disinfect them with white wine vinegar. Spray the vinegar onto the toys and allow them to dry.

Avoid buying these items

You shouldn't purchase certain items at thrift stores. Personally, I won't purchase underwear. It's not because it's unsafe, but I don't like the idea that someone else has worn underwear. As long as you can overlook the ick factor, there is not much to be concerned about.

Hard hats and helmets are important safety equipment that should be replaced regularly. Structures can be damaged if a helmet or hard hat has been subject to a strong impact. You may not be as safe as you need to when you wear safety gear. Make sure you always buy new safety gear.

To avoid bed bugs and fleas entering your home, make sure you only buy new mattresses and bedding. Infested mattresses from thrift stores can be home to bed bugs for up to six months. An infestation can be costly and you will want to eliminate them from your home.

Even if the makeup container looks brand new, never buy makeup from a thrift shop. Makeup can be ruined and packages may not have a use-by date. It's impossible to know the history of your make-up or where it has been. Therefore, it is better to spend more and get new stuff.

Although toys are fine to purchase, avoid stuffed animals. Stuffed animals can have been peed on, pooped on, or drooled on. They are difficult to clean. Spend more money to buy new stuffed animals. Wash any pre-owned stuffed animals you buy before your children play with them.

Although I recommend buying appliances, as long as it has been tested first, there is one appliance that you should avoid. Blenders can be difficult to clean and are full of food remnants. You can get a new blender for as low as twenty dollars

Shoes are another item that I would avoid unless they were brand new in their box. Comfortable shoes that have been worn in by someone else are not going to fit well. It is best to buy new shoes and then break them in.

Chapter 20: Write An Book On Your Hobby Or Profession

The internet is very vast and it has many resources that you can use easily for earning few more bucks. If you have any hobby or you have a great experience in your profession, or you just simply want to share your story with the world (like your survival story from any kind of disease), then you can earn good amount of money through writing a book a selling it on Amazon Kindle for a few bucks. E-books are becoming quite popular nowadays and if you have some skills to write one, then you can easily earn good income. Even if you are not good at writing, you can simply hire a professional ghost writer and pay him a little amount to write your story. Simply ask someone to make a recording about the topic you want to write and send it to the ghost writer to write an book for you. You can find many ghost writers on Fiverr and many other sites on the internet like it.

Write a Blog about Your Hobby or Profession

Some people have a great urge to write their day to day events in their journal diary. But why not to earn some amount for your habit, yes! You listened right, now you can earn few bucks for simply writing what you love to write on your blog. Blogging is becoming more famous day by day because real people like you and me share their day to day experience about a hobby or profession they love. There are many free blogging platforms like Blogger, Livejournal, or Quora where you can make your blog without even spending a dime and earn few bucks on your affiliate marketing links or Adsense advertisements.

You can also use Hubpages where you can write a blog on your favourite topic and Hubpages should pay you for the number of clicks on your webpage. This is called revenue sharing means they would share the Adsense revenue they should earn from your content page. Hubpages would be the best choice for you if you don't know blogging.

Join Some Direct Sales Business

Direct sales business is also a great way to earn good income. There are many companies worldwide that should provide you a chance to promote their product and earn good income. Many companies claim that their product is so good that it should sell automatically, but this is not the case in most of the direct sales business and you must know something about the product that you are going to promote. If you want to become a successful direct sales representative, then you must have some marketing skills like friendly, knowledgeable, and genuinely enthusiastic about the product you promote. Next, you must have a good connection with the product you promote, and you must love to buy or sell it.

You must do a thorough research about the product you are going to promote like you can ask the company manager some frequent questions to justify whether you are investing your money and time at right place or not. You can ask some formal questions like how much would it cost to begin the business? Does the company pay for any kind of promotional material like flyers and banners after you become a sales representative? Would it be necessary for you to buy the product or promotional material or you can just promote their product?

Do some research about the number of sales representative in your locality for the same product or company. Direct sales business is all about getting buyers in your locality and if there are many sales representatives already available in your locality, then you would not be able to make any profit and your investment will go waste. Try to find other options of selling or promote your product like eBay or craft shows. There are many sites available on the internet that should provide you a full insight about the direct sales and one such website is directsalescareers.com. So, ready to hustle and sell and make some profit with direct sales businesses.

Try Mystery Shopping

Mystery shopping is also becoming a popular trend among frugal living people who can save a lot of money on watching movies, shopping, playing, and many more. Check for the local company in your area or a company that provides mystery shopping opportunities in your area on the internet. Sign up for their account and they should inform you through an e-mail whenever there is any requirement for mystery shopping and the fun part of mystery shopping is you just have to what you generally do while shopping, but the company should pay you some amount for the merchandise you buy or for any movies you watch. This way, you can save a lot of money while doing the usual shopping at your nearest multiplex theatres and malls. Visit the allocated place and do review the products and services of the store or mall you visit and take some photos for the proof. On successful completion of your survey or review, the company should pay you the reimbursement for what you have spent at the store or mall. This is a great way not only to save but also enjoy your shopping.

Arrange Party for a Profit

Many companies are trying other options to promote their product. The advertising costs on TV and newspaper are increasing at a rapid rate and some small industries are looking for another way to promote their products. Many companies are arranging sponsored parties in some localities to attract the potential customers to their product. After all, nothing should be greater than just promoting your product on the go while the party is on full mood. Wouldn't it be wonderful for you to host a party that can give you more money than you spent? You can invite few vendors who represent different kinds of products so that they would set up a stall in your party for the promotion. Some companies are already involved in sponsoring parties and they should give you either free merchandise or 20% of the commission they earned from the night.

Ask each seller to invite a group of potential customers to your party. Get a general idea of how many people are coming so that you can arrange your seating and food properly. Invite at least one vendor who deals in food or beverages and could provide appetizers. This way, your effort will become less and you would only have to provide some drink.

Chapter 21: Cable/Internet

If you just moved or otherwise don't currently have cable and/or internet services, my advice is to simply shop around. You can read reviews online, but also ask people who they've used and what their experience has been. However, take any recommendations with a grain of salt, and if someone tells you that they hate X company, ask them why. One time I had a friend tell me that they didn't like Comcast because they took forever to come install the service, but it had to do with my friend never being home during the installation window. This led to Comcast having to reschedule the installation three different times and it's hardly Comcast's fault. Another friend complained that their provider just didn't have reliable signal, but they lived out in the woods and every provider had difficulty getting signal to them. Again, hardly the provider's fault. On the other hand, if you have multiple people in a metro area saying that they have problems with their service and the online reviews are along the same lines, then that's a red flag. No matter how cheap it might be, stay away from providers like that.

I must admit that I was never really tied to cable TV. I mostly watch things over the air or streamed online. However, my mom has had DirecTV and later on Comcast, enjoying their countless channels and seemingly never-ending options of shows and movies. The easiest way to save money with cable TV is by opening your bill and seeing the itemized charges. Can you spot anything that you can live without? Perhaps you added the Sports package in November because you didn't want to miss any NBA games but it's now July and there are no more games until November. In fact, you haven't touched any Sports channels for two weeks. Making a call to your provider to drop the Sports package will save you money over the next few months and only takes a couple of minutes. The same can be said for any of the added packages that you aren't using. Don't put off making that call. In fact, put this book down and call right now. The book will still be here, and you'll be in a better mood from knowing that you saved some moolah. The longer you wait, the more money you'll waste.

Another trick is simply calling up your current provider and asking politely if there's anything they can do to lower your monthly bill. I cannot emphasize enough how important it is to be polite to the service person, because ultimately they'll be deciding whether you get the perk or not. Yelling, belittling, and asking for a supervisor before even giving them a chance to help is rude and oftentimes ends with you not getting a deal. Some companies have internal specials that they're allowed to give existing customers in order to keep them as customers. If the agent knows about these, they'll usually try to use them right away if you mention that you are unhappy with the pricing or are thinking about switching providers. Sometimes you get a service representative that isn't as well versed in the different deals. Before asking for the manager, first ask if they have a Retentions Team they can transfer you to. This department's sole purpose is to convince you to stay. Again, your experience may differ depending on the seniority of the agent you get, but my experience has been very positive and they have offered me deals that I couldn't find anywhere on the company's website. There's been a couple of times that the agent has been so good that they figured out ways to combine promotions to give me bigger savings. Again, being nice to the person on the other end likely improved my odds of them going above and beyond.

I found out about the Retentions Team once when I was trying to cancel my service with Comcast. I was happy with the service, but I was moving out of the state and couldn't keep the service anymore. The agent transferred me to the Retentions Team, whose agent offered a promotional 12-month pricing that was $20 less than what I was currently paying.

That would have come out to savings of $240 over the year. At the end, I still closed my account but it was great knowing that I could ask for that team in the future if I was ever unhappy with my pricing.

Let's say that you are not in any contract and that your current provider says they don't have any deals they can offer you. Well, it's time to decide how much you are willing to do to save money. If you are interested in investing a little bit of time, then I recommend looking at what other providers in your area are offering. You can start by looking for specials online or calling to ask directly. Sometimes it helps if you tell them that you are with X company and are looking to change because your current bill is too high. It's not often, but sometimes there are unadvertised deals targeted solely for customers from X company moving to Y company. If you are considering changing providers, then you should have already looked at your itemized bill and should be familiar with the add-ons that the new provider will charge. Use this to your advantage and ask them about costs for TV boxes and installation, as doing so will avoid surprises later on. It doesn't hurt to ask if they can throw any of the add-ons for free. One time I simply asked if they could discount one of the three TV boxes we were getting, and they threw in the 3rd box for free. That was a savings of $10 per month or $120 per year.

Time for an exercise using numbers. This one is actually from my personal experience. I was nosing around my mom's bills when I noticed that she was paying nearly $280 for her Frontier/DirecTV package. I looked at the bill and saw that her promotional pricing for the internet had increased, that she had channels that nobody in the house watched, and that she was being charged for a TV box for a TV that broke a long time ago. I called Frontier and they actually refunded a couple of months for the box we hadn't been using (surprised me) and asked me to return it to avoid any future rental fees. As far as the promotional pricing, they told me they couldn't lower it any. Lastly, they informed me that they could take off the channels we weren't watching OR upgrade me to another package that had more channels but costs the same. BE CAREFUL WITH THE UPGRADE TACTIC! They are trained to word it in such a way that you'll want to say yes, but you should always ask for more information or whether you can call and add it later. Sometimes it's worth it, other times it isn't. You won't know until you do your research. In my case, there were no children in the house and the upgraded package was going to add some kid's channels and STARZ for free for 3 months (afterwards there would be a monthly fee for keeping STARZ). No thank you.

At that same time, Comcast was having a smoking deal where I could get faster internet, the channels my mom and siblings watched on a regular basis, the TV boxes, and modem/router for $150 per month. The only thing that I would be losing from the package was the land line, which was fine because I had been trying to convince my mom for months that it was time for a cellphone. Adding the landline was an extra $20 per month while the cellphone was going to be an extra $30 (for me it was worth it to pay $10 more for the cellphone service). The pricing was guaranteed to remain the same for 12 months, at which point it would be raised $30/month. I was advised to call them when the promotion expired since they value customer loyalty and often have other promotions for existing clients. Finally, they were upfront about charging a $95 activation fee.

Let's recap. I was faced with the option to remain with Frontier paying $280/month or move to Comcast where I would be paying $150 per month for a year. Moving to Comcast meant losing the land line (which wasn't that big of a deal since I could port that number to a cellphone for my mom) and getting faster internet speed. That's a savings of $130/month for 12 months for a total of $1,560. Let's not forget about the installation fee that would cost an extra $95 upfront.

Making this change still led to a savings of $1,560 - $95 = $1,465. It took me about 5 hours to cancel with Frontier, open the new account at a Comcast kiosk at the mall, and set up the installation of the new provider. Totally worth it if you ask me. That's $1,465 that my mom would have paid over the year if I hadn't intervened.

The last advice I am going to give regarding Internet is to think about buying a router instead of renting one from the company. They will try to convince you that it's best to rent it because if anything goes wrong they will give you a replacement at no cost. This is really up to you and your preferences. It's totally understandable if you don't want to deal with buying and installing the router on your own, but I figured I would write it in since this book is about tips on lowering your bills. Providers like Comcast use a router/modem combo, which you can buy without breaking the bank. They can cost about $100-$150 when new, but the advantage is that the equipment is yours. You can also try finding one on Craigslist, Nextdoor, or eBay for a much cheaper price (the downside is that you won't have a warranty). Again, this is a coin toss and either renting or buying is pretty equal at the end of the first year of having it. Savings from buying your own equipment become noticeable after about 14 months, depending on the cost of the rental. Normally, they will rent it to you for $10-$15 per month, which comes out to $120-$180 throughout year one or $200-$300 after two years. If the rental is $15 per month and the cable/modem costs $100 at the store, then you would be saving $80 in the first year by buying instead of renting.

Chapter 22: Clothing

Buy higher quality and more expensive clothing items

For items that you'll use for a longer period, like shoes, sweaters, coats and jackets it makes sense to splurge a little more up front and buy something that is of high quality. I'm not talking about spending $3,000 on a fur coat, I'm talking about spending $400 on a solid, warm, long lasting coat in comparison to a $150 one season only not-so-warm coat. In the long run, if you spend that extra money on something that is high quality, it'll last longer, make you look better and just be worthwhile overall. This is one of those times, spending more makes more financial sense.

You could divide the price of the item by the number of times you'll likely wear or use it. For example, with the $150 coat I used in the previous example, you might use it for one season or 30 times which is

$5 per use. The $400 coat you might use for 4 seasons or 120 times, which would be $3.33 per use. The key is to buy timeless pieces that you won't get sick of.

Spend less on clothing items that you go through quicker

On the other hand, it might make sense to spend much less of clothing items that you either spend less time wearing or get worn out quicker. Underwear, undershirts, t-shirts, and socks might be a few of those items. Obviously, it depends on how picky you are, but I'm sure more people notice a nice sweater over a nice pair of socks. Just saying.

Don't buy "Dry Clean only" clothes

The obvious reason, because you have to spend more money on dry cleaning to clean it, unless it's something that's somewhat of a necessity (read: suit for work) you probably don't need it.

Rent Expensive Occasional Clothing

If you're attending a party or an event that requires you to dress up, considering renting the piece of clothing that could cost you a few hundred dollars. You'll still look just as good. Check out sites like renttherunway.com.

Don't dry clean, iron your own shirts

I've been doing this for a long time, every week you go through at least 5 work shirts, if you spend $2 per shirt (probably more) then that's $10 per week. If you work say 45 weeks in a year, then you're spending $450 on dry cleaning your shirts. So which iPad did you want to buy again?

Repair your shoes instead of throwing them out

Spend the $20-25 to get your soles repaired instead of spending another $200 on a new pair of shoes. If you bought quality shoes, they should last for a very long time as long as you take decent care of them. They'll last even longer if you repair the soles and polish the shoes on a regular basis.

Buy second hand clothing

If you're ok buying second hand clothing then this will save you a lot of money, especially if you want different looks all the time. You can hit the local second hand shops, or you can try eBay or Craigslist for deals. You can even buy designer items at a steep discount with this method.

Look at consignment stores

Consignment stores are where people have the store sell their items and maintain ownership until the item is sold. Much like second hand shops these stores will have different inventory than the next store and are worth checking out if you're looking for something unique and a deal. You can also check out sites like thredup.com or liketwice.com for good solid second hand deals.

Buy out-of-season clothing

Buying out-of-season clothing is great since you'll find many usually expensive items at a steep discount. Buying a coat going into the spring or a short sleeve shirt going into the fall will save you money. To take this one step further buy pieces that are timeless. Sure there are fashion fads that will go out of style after one season or a year, but if you buy clothing items that last and don't go out of style, then you'll be saving heaps of money while looking great. Just because you're buying on sale doesn't mean that you are buying items that don't look good! But be selective! Which brings me to the next point...

Be wary of the outlet malls

Outlet malls are great. I love shopping at outlet malls because there are lot of deals that you just wouldn't find in the retail shops of all sorts of brand names. Burberry, Coach, Ralph Lauren and so on, but did you know that many items that are sold at outlet malls were made just for the outlet malls? And many products aren't a good deal at all, they seem like they are because you're at an outlet mall, something I like to call "the outlet effect." So do your homework before hitting the outlet malls!

Don't visit H&M, Zara, or Forever 21 to "check things out"

The $10-15 clothing item that you buy that you think is a complete steal might be, but if you don't wear it or only wear it a couple times it's not worth it. If you visit an H&M every week and spend an average of $20 every time you're dropping $1,040 a year. Don't you think you could have bought 2 to 3 amazingly quality clothing pieces for that price that could have lasted you for years?

Buy one awesome swimsuit

Here is one of the tips where I'll allow you to splurge. Buy a great quality and amazing looking swimsuit that will last you for years. I know many people that buy a new swimwear for every vacation they go on and this is honestly a huge waste of money. Unlike your daily clothing, unless you're always travelling with friends, no one will know if the swimwear that you are wearing is new or not. Buy one awesome swimsuit and use that for several vacations and you'll come out ahead in the long run.

Revive your favorite pair of jeans!

Before you look to buy a new pair of designer jeans because you think your absolutely favorite pair of jeans is all worn out, check out DenimTherapy.com. Get it repaired, revamped or even turned into shorts!

Make a list of all the clothing items you need!

Spend some time going through your wardrobe and find items that you actually need. And I mean really need, not replace for the sake of replacing. While you're at it, pick out items that you don't need and sell those off on eBay of other sites. Make a list of the items that you need and stick to them. This way when you go shopping, you know exactly what you're looking for and it won't be as easy to make impulse purchases.

Chapter 23: Budgeting, Saving And Planning

To survive living cheap you must know how much money is coming in, and how much is going out. Hopefully more is coming in than going out and you can save the difference. You do need some money in the bank for little things that sneak up on you, like car repairs and taxes. And I think the main goal of living cheap is to save some money. But in today's world you have to live cheap just to survive.

You should try to avoid fees, especially bank fees. I didn't realize it but my bank account had an overdraft limit. When I went into overdraft I didn't even know until I checked the account. The bank didn't send me an email or nothing, and I was overdrawn for a while. Then I got lumbered with a fee, so I marched into the bank and asked them to remove the overdraft. That is a thing they call an automatic overdraft to help you out of course, but also to boost their bottom line. I prefer cash to money in the bank. Another thing is credit cards. They are dangerous but necessary. I learnt very young just how dangerous they were. In the end I had to cut my credit cards up and close the account. Then I got lumbered with a close account fee which was not cheap. So now I only have one credit card which I use in times of emergency.

I use the simplest of budgets, Keep all receipts food, gas and what ever in a bag and then add them up at the end of the month. So I know how much is going out. I don't do very much impulse buying except at garage sales, and when I get home after garage sales I write down everything I brought. There are a few places that still take cash and I try to keep track of all cash going out.

On the other side of the ledger I keep track of everything that comes in. Most goes direct into the bank but things like brought on Facebook are still cash. I do try to save mainly for things that creep up on you.

Like the car breaking down and taxes, house and car. The taxes on the house run about $3000 and the car goes over $300 a year and I've got 2 cars, so I've got to save enough to keep the tax man happy.

I must live an incredibly boring life, I probably go out for one coffee a month and sometimes fast food when I am hungry and that is about it. Never go to the pub, just drink my homebrew wine and that keeps me going. My cheap treat is chocolate but I only buy when on special.

What To Do With Cars

Used cars are not expensive but getting them fixed can be very expensive. I only buy cars around 15 to 20 years old. I keep looking until the car I want comes along at the right price. If it is a small engine car I'm after, I just look at small engine cars. I try to never be in a situation where I have to buy. When I was sick of paying a $100 dollars to full up the car, I started looking at small engine cars with low mileage around 15 years old. I didn't know anything about small cars then, but now I know a lot. I lived on the internet and had alerts in my area for small cars. Then one came along. It had under a 100,000 kilometres on the clock and all the paper work was up to scratch. It just needed new tires and was around $3,000. We went to the bank and they wouldn't give me a loan, so I brought it on my credit card. Then I went back to the same back and asked them if I could get a loan to pay off my credit card. And they said "Yes" so I paid off the high interest credit card with a normal interest bank loan. Doing this gave me my credit card credit to fall back on.

This car costs just over $50 to fill up and goes further than the big car. I asked my back yard mechanic about tires and he said "No problem." He then went to the car wreckers and picked up 4 nearly brand new tires for about a third of the price to buy brand new. Then off to a fix it garage to get the tires put on. It didn't end there. About a month later the car needed a new battery, so off he went to the wreckers again, and picked up a near new battery for under half the new price. And so far that is about all the car has needed.

It is very handy to know a back yard mechanic, as they can save you a fortune. I buy the oil and the oil filter and he changes the oil for $30. Also when you need to get your car fixed and the back yard mechanic can't do it, it pays to shop around. My sister had a serious problem with her car and she got three quotes, ranging from $3.000 to $700. Now we have a real mechanic we can go to. Even my mechanic was surprised when she got it fixed for that price. And he didn't add anything onto the price. To find out who is a back yard mechanic, just ask around, someone will know somebody. That is the way now, just ask and you shall receive. I would say having the backyard mechanic has saved a lot of money and usually car bills are not cheap. So I would recommend getting to know one, and also having a network of friends who can do things.

People are very versatile, and there are people out there that will love to help for a bit of cash. It all boils down to asking around. I still have the big car and if anyone wants to borrow it, they just got to put some gas in it and they can have it. That has helped a lot of people and I can call on them if I need a hand. Networking doesn't just work for business. I have also surrounded myself with retired advisers, mainly to do with fixing the house. They tell me what products to buy, and what to do and how to do it. To keep things cheap you need a Do It Yourself mentality.

Also I shop around for gas or petrol as the price varies quite a lot from gas station to gas station. Now I have a fair idea who has the cheapest gas in my area, so I only buy gas there. And driving habits make a big difference. I don't drive hard or fast and I keep my foot off the metal. My sister was driving my car and I'm sure she drove about 100kms less than I do on a tank of gas. I was amazed at how far the car didn't go when she was driving. That was in the big car. She could only drive the automatic, not the manual car. So keep your foot off the floor and you will go a lot further on a tank. And at over $100 to fill her up you will go further.

Conclusion

Thank you again for downloading this book!

I hope you found this book helpful and effective in teaching you how to be frugal. May you have realized how important it is to be thrifty especially nowadays that it is very hard to earn money.

Don't forget to share your newfound knowledge to others and inspire your friends and family members to ditch the luxurious life and begin to live frugally.

Thank you and good luck!